HEART TO HEART

HEART TO HEART

THE ANATOMY OF A FOOTBALL CLUB

MIKE AITKEN AND WALLACE MERCER

SCOTTISH BREWERS

MAINSTREAM
PUBLISHING

First published in Great Britain in 1988 by
MAINSTREAM PUBLISHING COMPANY (EDINBURGH) LTD
7 Albany Street, Edinburgh EH1 3UG

British Cataloguing in Publication Data
    Aitken, Mike, *1952-*
    Heart to Heart: the anatomy of a football club.
    1. Scotland. Association football. Clubs.
    Heart of Midlothian Football Club, 1985-1986
    I. Title   II. Mercer, Wallace
    796.334'63'094134

ISBN 1-85158-140-5
ISBN 1-85158-141-3 Pbk

Typeset in 11 on 12pt Imprint by Bookworm Typesetting Ltd., Edinburgh
Printed in Great Britain by Billing & Sons Ltd, Worcester

CONTENTS

CHAPTER ONE   *The Professionals*   *13*

CHAPTER TWO   *A Family Affair*   *26*

CHAPTER THREE   *The Talk of the Toun*   *39*

CHAPTER FOUR   *Takeover*   *51*

CHAPTER FIVE   *Turned Down by McLean and*   *60*
                       Wallace

CHAPTER SIX   *Out of the Maelstrom*   *69*

CHAPTER SEVEN   *Almost There*   *78*

CHAPTER EIGHT   *The Players*   *90*

CHAPTER NINE   *Good Habits*   *97*

CHAPTER TEN   *For the Game's Sake*   *108*

CHAPTER ELEVEN   *The Sweeper*   *120*

CHAPTER TWELVE   *Labour of Love*   *129*

CHAPTER THIRTEEN   *We'll Support You Ever More*   *141*

CHAPTER FOURTEEN   *Spirited Progress*   *154*

CHAPTER FIFTEEN   *Through the Looking-Glass*   *168*

CHAPTER SIXTEEN   *Taking Stock*   *180*

CHAPTER SEVENTEEN   *Business Class*   *187*

CHAPTER EIGHTEEN   *Chairman's Report*   *195*

Grateful thanks to the *Scotsman* for the use of some illustrations in this book.

Heart to Heart is a collaborative effort between Mike Aitken and Wallace Mercer. The journalistic work was undertaken by Mike Aitken. Those chapters where Wallace Mercer outlines in his own words his views on Hearts, the future of the game etc. are clearly by-lined.

Tony Belfield

FOREWORD

A S THE SPONSORS of the competition at the time, I can recall finding myself on the pitch at Hampden at the infamous Scottish Cup final when mounted policemen were called upon to restore order. Mayhem disrupted what should have been a showpiece occasion. I would have taken some persuading that day that Scottish football in the 1980s was the proper vehicle to provide the right kind of image our company, Scottish Brewers, sought in a changing market-place.

Thanks to the Criminal Justice Act, however, which was years ahead of similar legislation in England, Scottish football cleaned up its act. Off the field the crowds came back in ever-increasing numbers. And on the field the standard of competitive play rose. Even top internationalists from England were attracted to play for the leading Scottish clubs.

This book tries to tell the story of the revival in Scottish football over the past six years or so when the Premier Division has established itself as the fastest-growing league in the world. It concentrates on events at Tynecastle since Wallace Mercer, one of a new breed of football businessmen, took over as chairman and helped to turn Hearts, Edinburgh's ugly duckling, into a swan.

But it also paints a broader picture of the present-day football scene and doesn't bring down the curtain at Hadrian's Wall – there are also illuminating contributions to be found in these pages from men like Irving Scholar, the chairman of Spurs, and Martin Edwards, the chairman of Manchester United.

Through our involvement with Rangers FC as sponsors with McEwan's Lager and through the Tartan Special Manager and Player of the Month awards, Scottish Brewers are significant investors in Scottish football. As shareholders at Tynecastle we are particularly pleased to be associated with *Heart to Heart*, a project which describes and analyses a great sporting success story in snapshot form.

Tony Belfield.
Managing Director, Scottish Brewers.

INTRODUCTION

I RVING SCHOLAR, the chairman of Tottenham Hotspur, thinks that what has taken place in Scottish football during the 1980s is a phenomenon unique in world football. This book is our attempt to do justice to a remarkable story of a remarkable club during these remarkable times. The genesis of the book lay in an invitation to write an updated history of Heart of Midlothian FC in 1986. In the aftermath of the club's twin near misses in League and Cup there were two chronicles of the team's achievements. However, it seemed to us two years on that a more innovative approach was required in order to set down the tale that needed to be told.

Heart to Heart is unique in a number of respects. It involves for the first time a partnership of a club chairman and a senior sports journalist to take the reader behind the scenes and supply an insider's view of the modern game. In addition this book, although it largely concerns itself with the cast of characters that populate one club – the players, the supporters, the administrators, the managers and the directors – strives to address a more general audience than is usual in such publications. We hope that what we have to say and report will be of interest to a broad spectrum of the football public.

The success story of Hearts in the 1980s is a mirror image for the success story of Scottish football, the fastest-growing league in the world. Our aim has been to examine and highlight a singular occurrence. Since 1981 attendances at Scottish League matches have increased by 1,871,606 or 79 per cent in seven years. During this same period Hearts' home gates have risen by almost 400 per cent, from 97,989 in 1981 to 365,929 in 1988.

Clearly, something extraordinary has been at work. This is a book about one club; but in dealing with issues common to all in the soccer industry, it attempts to be relevant to many.

Mike Aitken, Wallace Mercer.
Edinburgh, 1988.

CHAPTER ONE

The Professionals

MIKE AITKEN

I T IS the view of Lawrie McMenemy and of a number of other observers of the football scene that we live in a new age. For a time it was players that ruled the roost. Then the cult of the manager took over. Now it is club chairmen who regularly figure in the headlines. That analysis may be simplistic – quality players for instance have more power over their own destiny than ever before – but it does contain a kernel of truth. Namely, as David Murray, the owner of Murray International Metals and a Scottish entrepreneur with a variety of sporting links, has observed, that in the 1980s sport is big business and will only prosper when run along businesslike lines.

In 1987 the ICC publishing group produced a business ratio report on Britain's football clubs. It cost £125 and in terms of a popular read about soccer was never likely to pose a threat to the *Saint and Greavsie* annual. However, inside the blue covers of what was unpromisingly described as an industry sector analysis, were many facts and figures which lent some profound insights into the way that football has gone about its business in the 1980s.

In recent years, the buoyant nature of club football in Scotland has been in stark contrast to a period of stagnation in England. The reasons for this reversal in fortunes are numerous. Firstly, Scotland's legislators had the foresight to push through the introduction of the Premier Division. The reduced numbers in the top League served to increase competition. The public warmed to the new competition and 2,423,000 spectators watched the initial programme of matches in 1975/76. Attendances held firm at around the 2,200,000 mark until the early 1980s when gates dropped to 1,700,000 per season, which probably had something to do with Rangers' lack of success in the championship.

From 1981 onwards, Premier Division gates, and the total for Scottish football as a whole, have continued to increase. League attendances in 1988 were 19 per cent up on 1986 and reached a high of 3,677,193. There was no reason to suspect a drastic change in that trend as clubs such as Celtic, Hearts, Aberdeen, Dundee United and Hibs responded to the lead given by Rangers and invested in new, big name players.

"The spiralling influx of quality players, reversing the drain from north to south of the previous decade, undoubtedly had its effect at the box office," said Jim Farry, secretary of the Scottish League. "Crowds started to rise in 1981 and have maintained an upward graph ever since. By then the Premier Division had stabilised after reconstruction. And when freedom of contract came into effect that was another major contributory factor. Clubs began to see the necessity of putting their players on lengthy contracts and that kept the best of them in the Premier Division."

Irving Scholar, the chairman of Spurs, in a special interview for this book, expressed the personal opinion that what had happened in Scotland was unique in world football. "I think that Scotland have one of the furthest-viewing associations and leagues in the world. In my opinion, and this is strictly a personal view, I think that in the UK Scotland is 'way ahead of the English League. I think they've taken some monumental decisions – very brave decisions that have worked.

"I've got nothing but admiration for the people in Scotland and the way they handled a situation when the game had hit a low. They decided to do something drastic and address the problem. Now I read yet again for the seventh year running that attendances have risen once more. What's more, the rise is almost 19 per cent!

"There is no league in the world – and I feel very strongly about this – can boast of a record like that. Do you realise that England at the end of the 1987/88 season registered its second increase in a row? This was the first time this had happened since 1966. So you must give tremendous credit to what has happened in Scotland.

"What I find interesting is that people in football in England don't say someone somewhere has got it right, let's have a look at what they're doing and see if it will work for us. And there is no question in my view that in Scotland they've got it right. In Scotland they've created more

Rangers have spent millions in bringing personalities like Terry Butcher, Graeme Souness, Graham Roberts and Chris Woods to Ibrox – and Scottish Football has attained a higher profile as a result.

events and every game has some bearing either on the championship or relegation. Every game is a big game. The public want to see meaningful matches, not mid-table games. That's why I think the people who made the changes in Scotland happen deserve tremendous credit. But in England I'm not sure if you could get it to that point."

The reduction in the size of the Premier Division in 1988/89 to ten clubs with only one team relegated meant there were fewer matches to generate revenue. But there was no shortage of interest outwith the winning of the championship itself since half of the top ten were eligible for places in the three European competitions.

Whatever may have been said to the contrary by leading English clubs during the period of exile from European involvement to the effect that the cash from the UEFA matches was no big deal, the findings of the business ratio expert mentioned earlier were unequivocal on this subject: "The decline in sales for the First Division clubs is also reflected in a turnround with respect to profits. This subsector made pre-tax profits of £3 million and £4 million in 1983/84 and 1984/85 respectively but suffered a £3 million loss in 1985/86. These figures suggest it is still perfectly possible for football to be a profitable business even after years of apparent decline, but again the main emphasis is really on the crippling effect which the loss of European football has had for these clubs."

Martin Edwards, the chairman of Manchester United, who also agreed to a special interview for this book, reckons that England's absence from the European stage, coinciding as it did with the revival in Scotland, helped to focus national attention on what was happening in Scottish football. "Scotland has prospered while we've been out of Europe," he said. "The success of the Premier Division plus our absence from Europe was perfect timing."

The lack of involvement in club football on the Continent partly came about because the authorities south of the border did not apply themselves, as did their Scottish counterparts, to containing the problem of hooliganism at an early stage. It may have been unfair to blame Liverpool and English football for the tragedy in the Heysel Stadium, but if more had been done with regard to crowd safety and public order beforehand, the European authorities might not have been inclined to take as severe action as they did.

At any rate, the eventual return of European football in England, if and when it happens, should not be regarded as a panacea for all football's ills. The business analysts came to the same conclusion as many of the rest of us with the best interests of the game at heart when the question of League reconstruction was considered: "One characteristic of long or many-teamed divisions is the high proportion of matches . . . which will have no bearing on the championship race. For many spectators such matches have reduced appeal." This may be stating the blindingly obvious, but the need for changes in the way football is organised in England will not be satisfied by the simple expedient of shedding a couple of teams from the First Division.

While football has changed in recent years, it is a conservative industry by tradition. There is little enthusiasm at present for either ground-sharing or artificial pitches but progress on these fronts could in time lead to the kind of franchise system in operation in the USA.

If the English League is too unwieldy and the financial problems of the minnows pose a threat to the big fish – insolvency is not good for the image of the game – the business ratio report concludes about the Scottish League that while its financial difficulties are modest, "so also is the potential profitability." In other words there may be evidence to suggest that on a financial basis, Scotland's top clubs in time would also be better off in a British League, though this is not to take into account the host of other difficulties that might lie in the way of such a venture. But for the moment it is fair comment to suggest that if the possibility of a nationwide structure should arise, it will be in the main because a fall in profitability in England corresponded with a rise in Scotland.

In the list of the top ten clubs in Britain for profit margins, there are three Scottish clubs included, with Hearts in fourth place, reporting the highest annual sales growth of 38 per cent. It is an achievement, as this book will illustrate, that was reached by sound business practice off the field and astute management on it.

Clubs sell more than programmes these days – posters, ties, books, sweaters, records and calendars are just some of the merchandise available in the Hearts' shop.

The role of the club chairman, then, in the 1980s is bound to be of far greater significance and demand a much higher profile than in the past. When I met Irving Scholar, the chairman of Spurs, in his office at White Hart Lane, there were signs of ongoing activity in every corner of the room. In the course of a wide-ranging interview, fax messages came and went discreetly, mail was attended to and only the bank of telephones remained silent until our discussion was over.

A courteous, handsome 40-year-old entrepreneur who was very successful in the property market – his interest in Townsend Thoresen Properties ensured his personal wealth – before hitting the headlines with his takeover and subsequent stock-market flotation of Spurs, Scholar's knowledge of the football scene was impressive and his analysis of a changing environment was succinct.

"My experience over the past six years through speaking to many people in football, a number of whom have been chairmen or directors of clubs during the past 20 years, leads me to believe that the chairman's role has changed considerably," he began. "The business of football has altered since the early 1960s so that it is almost unrecognisable in form. That is due to a number of factors. The social fabric of the game has changed, in that 25 years ago the game was like a religion. I don't mean there was a sectarian involvement, but in the sense of a habit-forming part of life. People worked five full days and also on a Saturday morning. Here at Tottenham, it was very much an industrial area and there were factories, offices and warehouses all around the ground. What used to happen was that people worked until midday then popped into the pub, popped out again and into the football ground. In those days you might ask someone – are you going to Tottenham on Saturday? The answer would be yes. If you ask the same question today, the response will be – who are they playing? In other words, the bigger games now attract a larger audience, whereas 25 years ago even the teams that wouldn't be considered very attractive box-office today still achieved a very healthy turn-out."

I put it to Scholar that the spread of quality players was greater in that era and that the concentration of talent was now even more centred on the rich and powerful few.

"If you say that the big clubs are getting bigger, I would say to you that if you take Scotland as an example, the big clubs in the 1960s were Rangers and Celtic, who remain the big clubs today. The same is true in England where, strangely enough, the only addition to the big club league has been Liverpool FC. Liverpool were in the Second Division until 1961/2 when they were promoted with Leyton Orient. Everyone knows the story since then. Of course they were always a sizeable club and had a substantial following, but lacked success in the 1950s and were not in the top bracket.

"The other leading clubs – Everton, Manchester United, Arsenal, Tottenham – were big city clubs then and are still big city clubs now. They draw on a much wider audience than those teams that operate in a town rather than a city. And their position in the game hasn't altered. So, to go back to the original question, the chairman and directors 25 years ago would turn up at a match on a Saturday, have a few drinks, enjoy the football win, lose or draw and go home again after the match. Of course everyone wanted to win, but there were no additional pressures on them."

Martin Edwards, the chairman of arguably Britain's biggest club, agreed that the job of running a major club was much more complicated than in previous eras.

"I'm absolutely positive that the business of running a football club is more time-consuming and demanding than in the past. Now you can run a club one of two ways – either you have a paid chief executive, who doesn't necessarily need to be the chairman, but who will be there to run the day-to-day affairs, or you can have the chairman or owner of the club doing the job," he said.

"It then comes down to ability. I don't think it matters who does it provided that someone has the authority to run the show. In our case it works quite well. Some people think it is a bit unhealthy to be major shareholder, chairman and chief executive, but that depends on how you run the club, whether you run a democratic organisation or not. Now, at Old Trafford we do and the directors have every say. We agree the policy as a board and then I carry it out as chief executive. I'm not saying it would work in all cases but it does for us. I get involved in all the major things and probably in greater detail than most chairmen. But that's because I've got the time, and I'm paid to do so," he said.

Having looked at the changing role of the chairman, Irving Scholar went on to assess some of the changes on the playing side. "As to the players, if you look back to 1961, and I do believe that history repeats itself, Jimmy Greaves left Chelsea and went to AC Milan. Denis Law left Manchester City and went to Torino. And Joe Baker also went to Torino from Hibs. Obviously the money was great, but they didn't like the lifestyle and those players put their enjoyment of the game and their quality of life before cash," he said.

"Players today are far more worldly, far more cosmopolitan than they were then. But the same things apply. I'm convinced that when our players go abroad they do so for the money, they don't really enjoy it and, like most British people, don't travel well. They can't wait to get back home," he said.

The lure of foreign football is just one of numerous changes Scholar listed in the evolution of the modern British footballer. Freedom of contract has clearly made the most significant alteration of all.

"It has made the player master of his own destiny, and while I might not like it, I don't think it is wrong – if used correctly. When players take advantage of freedom of contract and what happened isn't in the interests of football, then I don't agree with that.

"Perhaps it is the game's fault that freedom of contract has never been fully explained to the public. In simplistic terms it means that whatever a player earns in salary, if a club doesn't offer at least what he was earning previously, then the player is automatically entitled to a free transfer. The player, at the end of a season when he is out of contract, can go and sign for anyone he wants without telling a soul. A fee is then agreed by negotiation between the two clubs or alternatively a tribunal. I'm told that there are not as many tribunal transfers as most people seem to think there are, but nonetheless they do happen, and most clubs have taken advantage of the system.

"In the old days of the retain and transfer system, it was only when the club agreed to sell a player that he got to leave. The other interesting thing about freedom of contract is that if the player decides to turn down your offer he doesn't have to sign a new contract, and yet the club must pay him his old salary in order to retain his registration and the right to receive a fee," he said.

Having pinpointed changes in the roles of players and chairmen and noted a significant shift in the balance of power between the two, Scholar turned to the commercialisation of football and the massive cash injection from outside sources.

"I was watching a video tape the other week of an FA Cup tie between Manchester United and Northampton. It was the day in the early 1970s when George Best scored a hatful of goals for United. What was interesting about it was that if you looked at the players' shirts, they were blank. Manchester United wore a plain red jersey. There wasn't even a club badge. Nowadays, of course, there is more than just a club badge, there is the manufacturer's logo and the sponsor's logo. So what has happened is that more and more money has been generated from outside the game because those companies like to be associated with someone and enjoy the exposure their product gets on television," he added.

The Spurs chairman is only too well aware that sponsors are not involved with football for altruistic reasons. He cited the example of Scottish Brewers' involvement with Rangers and how the presence of McEwan's Lager as the logo on the club's jerseys had helped the brewers' sales enormously. "We've been with our sponsor for five years. They're happy with us, we're happy with them, and in that sense it is like a marriage. It has given the company the exposure and the projection they wanted. We were one of the last major clubs to sign to a sponsor and we've renewed our deal with Holsten and are just about to start talking about another one. Their view is that it is a long-term thing and that a minimum period to make a sponsorship work is between seven and ten years."

Cash from commercial sources, however, has put extra pressure on clubs to succeed. Scholar also thinks that the circulation wars between the nation's tabloid newspapers has also had an effect on football. "These newspapers are all fighting for their market share, and football is a great product for them just as it is for television," he observed.

Given the amount of money that has poured into the game, as soap opera football at the top level probably has more in common now with *Dynasty* than *Coronation Street*. "Major clubs in England will now do a turnover approaching £4 or £5 million a year. A company doing that kind of business is no longer a corner shop. It is a big business and has to be run on sound business principles," said Scholar.

As to what the future holds, the chairman of Spurs cannot escape the conclusion that his job demands a full-time commitment. "There is no question about that. The demands are on you morning, noon and night. You can bet your life that the first telephone call in the morning will be about football, and that will set the pattern for the day until the last call at night before you go to sleep on the same subject.

"Running a football club is a very time-consuming operation. A former chairman of Tottenham, who is no longer with us, once told me that in his day he used to pop in on a Friday, say hello to everyone and sign a few cheques. He'd watch the match on a Saturday and there would be a board meeting once a month. If you look at the minutes of the old meetings you'll notice that they discussed everything in the most minute detail, from what colour the towels should be in the dressing-room to whether or not a light-bulb should be changed.

"Today a football club has to be organised along much more professional lines. This professionalism isn't just restricted to the boardroom, of course: it applies to the managers and coaches and the playing staff as well. When you read about Maradona being offered $1 million a year just to wear a certain manufacturer's football boots, it tells you what kind of potential there is," he said.

While the major clubs are rivals for honours, they also share common bonds of interest and Scholar can see those ties being strengthened in the years to come. "Your friends are your friends because you have something in common with them," he went on. "Football is no different in that respect from any other walk of life. I remember around five years ago when I'd only been involved with Tottenham for a very short period of time and the team was invited to compete in a tournament in Swaziland. Another English club, Manchester United, also went to Africa.

"I went to this tournament for a week with another Tottenham director; we lived in the same hotel as Manchester United, and obviously we mixed with their directors and manager. I must say it was an exceptionally good trip with a very friendly atmosphere between the clubs. I hadn't met the Manchester people before then but that trip cemented a great friendship of mine with Martin Edwards, the chairman of United.

"Martin and I were the two youngest chairmen in the First Division in England, and what was amusing was that over dinner one night in the hotel I recall vividly Martin and one of his directors discussing how they were going to resolve this problem and that problem. I looked round to the Tottenham director – and we both burst out laughing. I said that I thought we were the only ones who had those problems!

"The objectives of the bigger clubs are very similar and they think along similar lines. I'm talking commercially now, and whatever affects us will have repercussions for Liverpool, Manchester United, Arsenal and Everton. That will also be true for a lot of other First Division clubs, but perhaps to a greater degree for us."

The role of television will play an ever-increasing part in the finances of football, and it is fair to say that just as no one would be interested in coverage of the Scottish scene without Rangers, Celtic, Hearts, Aberdeen and Dundee United, the big five English clubs would decimate any deal south of the border if they withheld their involvement.

"I don't believe any television contract, whoever it is signed with, could be concluded without the top five clubs, because the television companies wouldn't be interested. I don't mean to sound either facetious or clever, but if you're talking about grade two I don't think they'd buy it. The same is true in Scotland where the absence of their top five would mean no deal.

"I'll say something else about Scotland for which I've got nothing but admiration. When they were being hit rather hard by the television companies insisting on live matches, I give them credit for holding off and saying 'No, we'll do one as an experiment'. In England there were ten experimental matches, but once the tests started they didn't change. In Scotland they created a scarcity, and when you get a situation like that, up goes the value."

The advent of cable and satellite television, of course, means that for the first time in Britain the network channels have serious competition. A couple of years ago in France a cable company bought the rights to 20 live matches. Up until then the French league got peanuts for television football. Suddenly they were getting £10 million for 20 games. On top of that, matches were sold in packages to the networks.

"If that's going to happen in England, then not only is the initial sum higher but also, even more interesting, is the money that is generated by football – i.e. the advertising around a programme. The Football League will get a percentage of that as well. Plus, and this is also something for the future, pay-TV will beam in on live football in mid-week rather than weekends.

"The pay per view sector, say for Liverpool versus Manchester United on a Tuesday evening, will cost £2 or £3 to actually watch the programme. Football will get 50% of that revenue. In terms of numbers it throws the whole existing operation right out of the window. The deal has enormous potential. Let's say a million homes watch the match and each home pays £3. For one game only, football will get £1.5 million plus the rights fees and the share of the advertising and the board advertising. That's something to think about for the future," he said.

While this book strives to tell the success story of Scottish football through the renaissance of one club, Hearts, Scholar would like nothing better than to see the Scottish revival duplicated in England. "We have to look at Scotland and the way things are done there," he said. "That system of a Premier Division, if it was formed in England along similar lines, with the clubs playing each other twice at home in a season – Liverpool would play Manchester United once at Old Trafford and once at Anfield before Christmas and the fixtures would then be reversed after Christmas – isn't something the public are going to complain about."

"If England copied the blueprint of the Scottish system then, personally, I believe that attendances in that division would go to somewhere near where they were in the late 1950s and early 1960s," he said.

Martin Edwards doesn't disagree with Scholar's analysis but is dubious about the likelihood of achieving such change. "I can see the advantage of a Premier Division-style league, but the problem with all these things is how do you go about it? I can't see it coming about in England by natural causes," he said.

The Manchester United chairman, however, remains a firm advocate of a British Cup involving the leading sides on both sides of the border. "We are very keen to have a British Cup, and when we spoke to our colleagues in Scotland at the time they also sounded keen. But it got brushed under the table, mainly because of the attitude of the Scottish Football Association. They were reluctant to get involved in matches with English clubs in case there was any trouble and that might jeopardise their place in European competitions – something the Scots enjoy and we don't.

"I also think that the Scottish League were against it for similar reasons. But yes, we would welcome a British Cup. We've got our First Division down by four games a season, so there are free dates and

Wallace Mercer is one of the new breed of club chairmen who understand that football is part of the entertainment industry. Here he meets Jim Kerr of Simple Minds.

there is room for it. If the Scottish clubs were interested, then I'm absolutely certain that type of competition could go ahead – but on this one the stumbling-block is Scotland rather than England," he said.

On the other hand, Edwards is more sceptical about the concept of a European league. This was the original vision of Gabriel Hanot in 1934 and found new life when the chairmen of Real Madrid and AC Milan, Silvio Burlosconi and Raymon Mendoza, asked UEFA to consider playing the European Cup on a sectional basis.

"I'm less hopeful of a European league," the Manchester United chairman acknowledged, "because then you start running across European associations and I don't think a mid-week European league would work. It would have to be all or nothing. I'm not sure the British supporter wants to see Spanish or Italian football. I think the one thing the supporters do get out of our game is entertainment. It is a different, faster game. I think if it came down to watching very negative football every week – and they'll put up with it in the European competitions because that's not the bread and butter – our people wouldn't have it."

Out of the same mould as Edwards and Scholar, Wallace Mercer is one of the new breed of club chairmen who understand that football is part of the entertainment industry. He is a character like Phineas T. Barnum, whose great gift lies in drumming up business for the circus but who knows whatever may be said to the contrary, the greatest show on earth is nothing without its players.

CHAPTER TWO

A *Family Affair*

WALLACE MERCER

A NY FOOTBALL CLUB is the sum of its parts, and it goes without saying that the most important people are the players. They are the key to the success of the operation. Everything else, at the end of the day, is just window-dressing. Many individuals, however, work behind the scenes, and in order to understand how a club functions, as well as its character, it is worth discovering a little about the personalities involved in the day-to-day operation. As the chairman of Hearts I knew how important it was to pick the right team off the field as well as to enable the managers to select a winning team on the field. The process wasn't achieved overnight, and since I took over control of Hearts I've learned a lot about myself as well as the running of a football club.

After being involved for some time as the major shareholder and chief executive overseeing the whole operation, I've realised that I would have to truthfully describe myself as a controlled egomaniac. I didn't know as much when I took on the responsibility for guiding Hearts' affairs, but I'm also a person who enjoys show business – and I suppose you could call me an impresario. In other words, football has given me a stage on which to tailor an act that can cope with the more excessive aspects of my personality. I think that this side of things has developed over the years, and it may be significant that my personality has undergone changes in tandem with the development of Hearts. If I'm being quite honest, I'd have to say that one has fed off the other.

26

I believe that I've attracted the limelight back to the club for the right reasons – before I took over most of the publicity was bad – and, of course, I enjoy being involved with the media. If I've done anything for Hearts, I would be the first to admit that the club also gave me a platform. There's no doubt that in the formative years I was prepared to beat the drum and seek attention for attention's sake in order to try and help open up the club again. Quite simply, Hearts needed an improved reputation as well as higher status. What happened was that, with the passing of time, I was able to adopt a more conservative approach. In a sense I'm now what the media like to describe as an "established personality". By that I mean that I will get coverage on the merit of what I have to say, or, more importantly, for what the club have achieved. It used to be that Wallace Mercer did most of the talking for Hearts. Now it is the football team who do that.

If I was to be asked what the ideal chairman of a football club should be like as we look ahead to the 1990s, I would say that he must be a promoter of his business. This is happening in industry, banking and politics, where politicians are packaged through the media as never before. Given these developments, all that Wallace Mercer and Hearts have done is to be aware of the coming change in the market and perhaps anticipate trends that have helped us to project the business.

To some extent I am quite ruthless in promoting myself, because I know there is a spin-off for the business. If you are going to be chairman of a football club, by definition, I don't think you can be a shrinking violet. It is the kind of job that automatically will attract larger than life characters. Football is show business. It is light relief from the more serious and fundamental issues that confront our society, like social deprivation and unemployment. It offers a balance on the back page of the newspapers, where sport still throws up heroes and villains, winners and losers, to the sombre, more complicated stories that fill the front page.

The longer I've been involved in football, the more I've become convinced that the game is an extension of the entertainment world. So that is the primary function of how I see the chairman's job – to promote his club – and at Tynecastle I've been fortunate in having a board of directors who are willing to help manage the business and support me. They know that I am the up-front communicator and salesman. The Hearts board are not a group of 'yes' men, however. I am aware of my own tendency to go over the top, and the directors were hand-picked by me to control some of the more excessive things I'm inclined to get involved in at times.

There is an effective system of checks and balances at Tynecastle, though I'm only fully aware of this six years into the exercise. When I took over Hearts the club got a lot of attention, but for all the wrong reasons. Now it earns coverage on merit – because the business is doing well. In that sense it is quite a different organisation to run from the one that we started with. I think that if you are going to compete with Rangers, Celtic, Manchester United and Spurs, then you have to give the people who are going to come along and support you – who want to believe in the club anyway – a sense of leadership. Half the battle, in my opinion, is to provide that.

In the fullness of time – and I intend to return to the topic later in this book – it is my view that a British league will come about. When that happens, then chairmen, or chief executives, will act on a full-time basis for their clubs. The way things are going, the top clubs require a major commitment from whoever is in command. He needs a specialised skill in business, management and communication. It is not the case that the running of a club can be left to the secretary and a range of other individuals. A football club needs someone who can give it a prime directive – and that is certainly not the province of managers or coaches whose knowledge and understanding lies primarily with the game of football. Just because someone was good at playing football or has a knack of putting a team together doesn't mean they have an awareness of the business or commercial side of the operation.

If you take someone like David Holmes, who is chief executive of the Lawrence Group and chief executive of Rangers, the time may come when the priorities are reversed and it is the football club that takes up more of his time than the other bits and pieces of the business. Glasgow Rangers FC are such an important element in the Lawrence Group that the management of the club could eventually come first.

The same applies in England where a man such as Irving Scholar at Tottenham Hotspur, while he continues to develop his property empire, will want to direct most of his entrepreneurial attention to the football club if Spurs are to be commercially successful in the broader sense.

That is also very much the case with Wallace Mercer. The amount of attention I devote to Hearts' business affairs now is far greater than I gave six years ago. Then, I contributed a lot of direct management attention in terms of decisions – but what I'm doing now, bearing in mind that it is a more complicated as well as a more competitive industry, is spending a lot more time considering the longer-term strategic planning of Hearts. And that is much harder to do than just the routine questions of 'do we buy him?', 'should we sack him?', or 'what about this contract?' that have to be answered each season.

When I go on holiday in the winter months to Florida, at least half my time is spent planning the business affairs of Hearts. I meet my colleagues on the board when I come back and we discuss the way ahead. However, the onus is on me to create the options and formulate the agenda. Then the directors can give their opinion.

In Scottish football, and perhaps this is true to some extent in England as well, more power is invested in the major clubs than ever before. It is a situation where the rich are getting richer and will continue to do so. By definition, the difference between being a full-time professional club with ambition and the rest has grown significantly. Even in the Premier Division there is a difference, and two leagues exist within that championship. The professionalism of the leading clubs sets them apart from the others. Celtic, Rangers, Aberdeen, and, to a lesser extent, Hearts, are managing and developing their affairs on a scale that is more substantial than the rest.

As I said at the outset, however, no club is a one-man organisation. I go back to 1981 when I had to restructure the board and appointed directors who would truly help me to run the business. The only man from the previous régime who had any merit at all as far as I was concerned was Bobby Parker. I'm a great believer in the tradition of a football club, and Bobby offered us a link with the past, having been an important player during the golden days of the 1950s. He was once chairman in his own right and has been a good soldier in my time.

Although Bobby was a first-class captain on the field of play, in his time as chairman he wasn't a successful communicator. Bobby was a prime example of a knowledgeable football man who wasn't able to put over the message to the media. Nowadays, Bobby's main role at the club is a social one. It is his job to look after the boardroom on match days and entertain our guests from other clubs. Politically, it is a very important role. Bobby also attends reserve matches and represents the club in the community, whether it be at funerals or whatever. He links the past to the present and is a sound adviser to me on football matters.

Bobby has sat beside me at every first-team game I've seen Hearts play. He's had good counsel to offer, and in my early years as chairman he was able to outline situations that he'd seen crop up before. To begin with, I had a tendency to react to particular situations like a supporter. Bobby would say, "Wallace, that's the way you should look at it" — because for him it was a case of *déja vu*.

It was always my view that the board needed a presence from outwith the area of Edinburgh and the Lothians to give us a broader perspective. We wanted a base that would at least reflect the central belt in Scotland. Douglas Park, who hails from Hamilton and is the owner of the largest private bus company in Scotland, had been a supporter of Scottish football for some time. He was a well-known face on the SFA's foreign trips and had been a sought-after director by a number of clubs over the years.

Douglas was the same age as myself and agreed to come on to the Hearts board, buying some of my shares and being prepared to make a contribution. Like Bobby, Douglas is not a natural communicator, and in some respects our relationship isn't always plain sailing. I've got a diametrically opposed style to Douglas Park and no one would take us for two peas out of the same pod. On his own merit, though, Douglas runs a highly successful business empire, and in order for us to co-exist on the Hearts board there has to be give and take on both sides. Suffice it to say that now we've both been on the board for nearly six years.

Of course, Douglas has brought other elements to the business, such as the private bus transport of fans to away matches. It was something we instigated more than five years ago and was quite unique to Scottish football at the time. On top of that he's had a part to play in our commercial activities and various other political matters, where having a colleague with a base in the west of Scotland was important.

Pilmar Smith is a different type altogether. He is the archetypal Hearts supporter who has done well for himself. Pilmar is a self-employed bookmaker, and as a bachelor he finds the time to visit Tynecastle most days. A lifelong follower of the club, Pilmar is not the kind of man you could con with sweet words or clever sayings. I appointed him to the board, not just because he was a shareholder and an individual who cared about the club. He was also a man who had seen what had happened to Hearts over the course of 30-odd years and felt the supporters deserved better. Pilmar was brought in to do a specific job – and that was to look after the interests of our supporters and represent them in the boardroom.

It had struck me as odd, to say the least, that while most clubs had links with the playing side and links with the business world, no one gave much thought to the most important people of all, namely the customers who come and pay their money to watch the team, week in and week out.

There was no way that Wallace Mercer, with his particular A1 profile, living in a smart house at Barnton, could pretend to be a

New faces were needed in the boardroom and I was delighted in 1982 to welcome directors Douglas Park (left) and Pilmar Smith to Tynecastle.

punters' man. I'm not, either in an economic or a social sense, and it would have been hypocritical of me to have suggested otherwise. I have a sympathy and an empathy with them, but that's a different matter.

Pilmar was my first appointment, and a very successful one it turned out to be. His contribution has developed over the years, and in the fight against hooliganism he helped with things like the introduction of video cameras. It is a remarkable fact that Hearts have reduced their police costs – per unit in relation to the running of the business – in every year since Pilmar joined the board.

Pilmar Smith also has strong connections with the Labour Party and that political dimension has introduced a new avenue of openings for the club. Our contacts have been national as well as local through men like Alex Kitson and Neil Kinnock. On top of all that, the substantial refurbishing and renovation work done at Tynecastle has been supervised by Pilmar during the past six years. Finally, he's a man that the players will talk to much more readily than to me – and in that sense there's an open connection between the views of the playing staff and the direction coming from the boardroom.

Sharing a joke with Neil Kinnock, the leader of the Labour Party, during a match against Falkirk at Brockville.

To sum up, I would describe the running of Hearts as a democratic autocracy. I own the major shareholding in the club – but it has never been used as Wallace Mercer's toy. Smith, Parker and Park are all self-made men who are quite capable of speaking their minds. They're not the types to be railroaded into supporting me on every issue.

In the six years we've been together as a group there hasn't been a major decision taken where the voting of the board wasn't unanimous. We debate matters around our boardroom table and I go with the broad consensus of opinion. In other words, we can all take quite different positions on various topics. Pilmar Smith and Douglas Park will see things at times from a quite divergent viewpoint from the one I hold. And I believe those differences can only be of benefit to the other 750 shareholders who are not represented on the board.

For I have to admit that Wallace Mercer without control and reins will ride roughshod over everything. I'm the type who will say, "There's 'a', 'b', 'c', 'd', that's what's going to happen." I regard my boardroom colleagues as my best enemies as well as my best friends. In a sense we've all grown up together, and are closer now than when we first started. I respect them all individually as men – even if sometimes they can be a pain in the neck. And I say that with tongue ever so slightly in cheek, because I'm the type who can sometimes find a democracy a pain in the neck.

More seriously, it is vital to have a unified board of directors since I believe that the players and managers know very quickly if there is a chink in the armour and one director is more willing to be supportive in their individual difficulties than the others or wants to get too close to players. This can be a major problem at any club. All my directors know what is expected of them and there are obligations they have to meet. On these matters I'm quite stringent.

As far as the day to day administration of the club is concerned, our secretary, Les Porteous, is a solid, reliable individual who used to work in the coal industry. He lives in a community where his status as club secretary of Hearts counts for much. He had some experience with Newtongrange Star before coming to Tynecastle in 1980 and has supplied a very loyal and constructive service to the club.

The parameters of Les's job mean that we expect no more from him than he is capable of achieving. I suppose it is true to say that when the rest of us are long gone Les will still be at Tynecastle. He was here before my time and no doubt will still be here after I've left. A club secretary, in my opinion, has to be the eyes and the ears of the chairman. And at this club Les has to mollycoddle the managers and do all their paper work for them.

At Tynecastle, Alex MacDonald and Sandy Jardine don't have any responsibilities other than the managing of the football team. They look after the club's most important asset in an emotional and a physical sense – the playing staff. In our structure, the club secretary, following the board's directives, runs the everyday business and looks after the interests of the managers.

There are three managers at Tynecastle: Wallace Mercer in the boardroom and Alex MacDonald and Sandy Jardine on the playing side. It is a little unusual for a club to have co-managers and the position was partly inherited. We were the first big club in Britain to appoint a player-manager – Alex MacDonald. I don't look back on that decision and try to claim any creative flair on my part for the appointment. The fact was that after spending a lot of money and realising that the manager of the day wasn't going to make it, even I understood that a new man coming in would have to reach the conclusion that half the playing staff weren't up to much and would want to replace them with new signings. We simply didn't have the money to do that. That's why a tier of management was eliminated. I took on Alex MacDonald as a senior professional and decided that he and I would learn the business together. Nothing gave me greater pride than the day when Alex was made Scotland's manager of the year, because we'd been together since day one.

Over the years Alex has developed as an individual and is indisputably an outstanding coach. He's not interested in the business side at all and figures are as much beyond him today as they were when he was first appointed. Ironically, Alex runs his personal affairs very prudently and deserves great credit for the way he's handled his career. Alex MacDonald doesn't want to move on a stage – although in five years' time he could surprise me – and in some respects still sees himself as one of the playing staff. I'm delighted with that because in the role of coach there's no one around to touch him.

Sandy Jardine was brought on board to try and expand the range of the management team. As a player he had a higher pedigree, although the careers of both Jardine and MacDonald were intertwined at Ibrox. What I've found as their partnership has developed is that the pair are like ham and eggs: you can't really have one without the other.

On their own, neither individual would fit the profile of the perfect Hearts manager. But then I have to admit that I've been spoiled in having the two of them. What I've got is a mix of two good friends and complementary personalities. They combine a number of attitudes and approaches – Jardine brings a touch of arrogance from his career status and more of a visionary approach, while MacDonald brings the grit, determination and ruthlessness. Between the pair I think I've got the ideal blend. When Jardine was given the opportunity to go to Aberdeen as manager there was no doubt that I had to create a régime that gave

I have the greatest admiration for Alex Macdonald as a coach and my proudest moment as chairman came when Alex was voted Scotland's manager of the year.

space to both of them. Hence their status as co-managers.

In effect, what this means is that MacDonald will continue as the coach – in that sense he is Hearts' manager – because to my mind MacDonald is the best coach in Scotland. Jardine, who retired from playing in 1987, has skills to offer in other areas. He fronts the junior club and has been involved in other business matters with me – as a former captain of his country Jardine carries a high profile – and in future the pair will develop along different lines.

What I have to give the most serious consideration to is the future of the club, and the way MacDonald and Jardine progress is vital in that context. If I was to be quite blunt about the make-up of the existing board, there is no one who could automatically take over the reins as chairman. I'm not discrediting Douglas Park, Pilmar Smith and Bobby Parker, who all have a contribution to make. But a different personality is needed to run the business. With the development of Alex MacDonald and Sandy Jardine – bearing in mind that perpetuity is part of my job – I hope to get the best of both worlds.

As far as the commercial side is concerned, during the first four years of my time with Hearts, Robin Fry was the commercial director and together, I think I can say in all modesty, we made a vital contribution to the club. We took over Hearts when they were in deep decline. Robin and I were both young men, a little naïve perhaps, but with absolute confidence in our abilities. We were one of the first in Scotland to get a shirt sponsor, the first to set up business clubs and various other innovations that have now been copied by others, sometimes on a grander scale.

Robin and I sold Hearts just as you might sell washing machines. It was absolutely crazy stuff – but we would try anything to dig the club out of the difficulties it was in. However, last year we found that the idealism had become excessive, the overheads were out of proportion and it was time to make some fundamental changes. Charles Burnett, who had been the number two, took over, and Robin went on to pastures new. We now have a very effective commercial unit. The primary aims are to maintain our lottery, to develop all our activities off the field and in general terms to earn, after all costs, around £400,000 in revenue in 1988. It may not compare with clubs like Manchester United, Liverpool and Rangers, but is still a substantial sum.

It is a fact that the leading clubs in Scotland are not only taking a bigger share of the cake from increased numbers going through the turnstiles but also from their off the field enterprises – this is what sets a club like Hearts apart from those such as St Mirren, Motherwell and the rest. We have a lot of staff employed on the commercial side and Charles Burnett reports direct to me as chief executive. My job is not only that of chairman. I'm responsible for financial planning, dealing with the cash-flow situation and reporting to the bank. I negotiate all the key contracts with the players. I have power of attorney in all the major commercial transactions. The commercial manager reports to me and at any given time I know the level of credit and debit. Given all that, it is clear that the club is run by Wallace Mercer – albeit with excellent support from Les Porteous, Charles Burnett, Alex MacDonald, Sandy Jardine and Pilmar Smith.

On the playing side, there are half-a-dozen individuals who stand out. The senior professional is Sandy Clark, who makes an important contribution off the field as well as on it. It is important to have someone in the dressing-room who has been to other places and seen different things and can advise the younger ones. Walter Kidd, the club captain, is also a valuable experienced servant. In my time we've always had players of their calibre, from Jimmy Bone and Willie Johnston onwards. Eamonn Bannon one of our most recent signings will also come into this category.

Here are Sandy Clark (left) and Craig Levein with the management team and myself after signing new contracts.

Hearts used to be known as a "Dad's Army" team, but we've moved on since the days when all our best players were in their 30s. Now we have an important group of young men in their 20s who are knocking on the door of the international team. Young players like John Colquhoun, who is also chairman of the Scottish Players' Union, Craig Levein, Dave McPherson and Gary Mackay all have a status that reflects well on them as individuals as well as the club. Behind the scenes, there are many full-time individuals who can't all be mentioned, as well as numerous part-time and, in some cases unpaid, contributors who help out because of their affection for the club. These people range from our sprint coaches George McNeill and Bert Logan to Alan Rae, who runs the physiotherapy department at Edinburgh's Royal Infirmary Hospital. There are numerous specialists in their own area who have an important contribution to make – men like John Binnie, who is an accountant with Lothian Region, and does a first-class job with our reserves. All these individuals want to be involved with Hearts and care for the club. It is a blend of individuals – think of our groundsman Willie Montgomery who has been here for more than 30 years and has seen them all come and go – which adds up to the Hearts family.

CHAPTER THREE

The Talk of the Toun

MIKE AITKEN

I T IS ONE of the puzzles of the history of Hearts that not only was the club unable to sustain the success of the 1950s and early 1960s, but that the fall from grace in the era that followed was so spectacular. Few individuals are as well placed to comment on what went wrong at Tynecastle as Bobby Parker. The former chairman has been connected with Hearts in one capacity or another since 1946, captaining the League Cup-winning team against Motherwell; taking charge of the third team and the reserves in the 1960s as well as serving on the board since 1970.

Parker believes that when Tommy Walker, one of the last of the gentlemen managers, stood down, the club made a serious mistake in giving the job to the long-serving coach, Johnny Harvey. Indeed, at the time, Parker advised Harvey – the man the players regarded as the motivating force behind the success story of the 1950s – not to take the post. "I told Johnny I didn't think he was built for the job," Parker recalled. "He was an excellent trainer and no one was better at lifting the players' morale. John was a nice guy and I was concerned that he maybe wasn't strong enough for the top post. He didn't like to upset people, and managers have to do that sometimes."

If Harvey lacked the ruthless streak Hearts needed to make changes in the wake of the disappointment of losing the championship to Kilmarnock in 1965 – one of the most traumatic events ever at Tynecastle – Parker felt that whatever the merits of the second-in-command, the club needed a fresh start after Walker's lengthy reign. "We needed a new face," Parker said. "Every club does every so often. A new broom needs to come in and change the attitude and the style."

Hearts didn't get the change of direction at the top that Parker felt was necessary. On top of this the club lacked cash to buy quality players – what little profits were made in the 1950s went on ground improvements at Tynecastle – and found itself bereft of talented youngsters. In this respect the dark days of the late 1960s and 1970s had their beginnings in Hearts' heyday. "The third team was full of old players," Parker remembered. "We played in the border league and won it – but we didn't have any young men coming through. The club needed kids for the future but it didn't groom them."

By the time Parker was invited to join the board in the spring of 1970 the club's fortunes were in serious decline – a state of affairs he began to understand when he attended his first directors' meeting. "I was sitting at the end of the table, opposite the chairman, not really sure what was expected of me. I looked up and I saw two of the older directors snoozing. Their eyes were shut, and being charitable I wondered if they were just gathering their thoughts. But after watching them for a bit I knew they were asleep."

The combination of an elderly board and lack of funds deepened the club's problems. "We needed a rich man to come in and change things, someone like Wallace Mercer to give the place a bit of leadership. But that wasn't possible until the constitution was changed. Before then all the shareholders thought they should be directors. You could only hold a limited number of shares and that led to the formation of cliques. There was rivalry amongst the shareholders and everyone thought they could do the job better than the directors. But when new people came on, they would soon say we didn't realise you had this to do and we didn't know about police bills and so on. Until the share issue took place, it wasn't possible to get in a businessman who was prepared to take a chance. There's no doubt that Wallace Mercer was exactly what the club needed. I backed Mercer during the takeover campaign because I was genuinely concerned that Hearts might be shut down and there would be just one club in Edinburgh."

That prospect alarmed many more people than Bobby Parker. Since the club was founded in the 1870s, the inhabitants of Scotland's capital city have regarded the Hearts as part of the fabric of Edinburgh life. The club is a social institution, albeit one that has been rebuked as often as it has been revered. The event that bonded club and city more closely than any other took place in 1914 when the Hearts side of the day

volunteered to a man for service in the First World War. Alexander
Irvine, a former chairman of Hearts, recalled in the foreword to Albert
Mackie's history of the club published nearly 30 years ago: "We also
remember with pride the action of the Hearts players in joining the
colours *en bloc* and forming the nucleus of the 16th (Sir George
McCrae's) battalion, the Royal Scots. That was one of the finest teams
Hearts ever had. Their action was a great stimulant to recruiting, which
was then on a voluntary basis. Four of the first team made the supreme
sacrifice. The memorial at Haymarket tells its own story of this great
chapter in the history of the team, and also of the players and members
who served their country in the Second World War."

To this day the clock at Haymarket, near the station, stands as a
reminder of Hearts' place in the community. Each year on
Remembrance Sunday the club attend a service at the memorial. A full
turnout is expected, and when Andy Roxburgh, the Scotland coach,
wanted to contact Gary Mackay to call him into an international squad
in 1987, the first the player knew of his promotion came when a message
was passed via Wallace Mercer's car phone to the player at the
service.

Of the teams that remain a part of the Scottish League today, only
Queen's Park, Kilmarnock, Hamilton, Dumbarton and Rangers can lay
claim to a longer history than Hearts. The Edinburgh club was founded
in the early 1870s when the colours were red, white and blue, jerseys
were described as sweaters and pants were worn long. The game was
purely an amateur affair in those days and Albert Mackie recounted
how players had to be prepared to dig deep into their own pockets. "The
players did not pay only their own personal expenses," he wrote. "They
also entertained the members of the visiting teams. Each man paid for
himself and for one of the opposing eleven. Entertainment after the
game was strictly teetotal. Fuller's and Buchanan's Temperance hotels
were usually the venues. On special occasions there was a spread in
Ritchie's in Cockburn Street. There was no systematic training for a
game, and a rub with a towel after a match was the nearest thing to a
massage. Some 'fatal colds' were attributed to men putting their clothes
on over their wet, uncomfortable flannels after the game."

Edinburgh was a rugby city at this time – some would say it still is as
far as the establishment is concerned – and while the likes of the Accies
and the Wanderers were in full cry, a Hearts team of sorts was founded
in 1873, though it was not until the following year that the club
amalgamated with the St Andrew Boys Club, who played at the
Meadows. The St Andrew club seem to have had the edge on players,

having defeated and dismayed the Hearts team of the day to such an extent that a marriage between the two was sought by the senior Hearts players. What Hearts principally had to offer, of course, was a great name – that of the Heart of Midlothian football club. After the merger both sets of players began afresh and sent their jerseys to be dyed. The new club colour was maroon and the mother of one of the players bought a piece of red crimson cloth and stitched eleven heart-shaped crests on to the jerseys.

There was no one explanation of where Hearts got their name, as Mackie colourfully recounted: "One version is that there was a dance hall known as the Heart of Midlothian in a place off the Royal Mile known as Washington Green Court. Some of the youths who frequented it stood joking with a policeman at the Tron Kirk. The policeman, ribbing them about their dancing, suggested they would be better employed kicking a ball about the Meadows. About 40 youths who frequented the dance hall clubbed together and purchased a ball, thereafter founding the football club and naming it after their favourite dance hall."

Perhaps the story of the club relying on the enthusiasm of these 19th-century casuals had too many coincidences to be entirely convincing. An alternative theory put up was that the club originated with the boys who played street football near the jail known as the Heart of Midlothian. This was pulled down in 1817, leaving a large heraldic heart in the causeway stones near St Giles' Cathedral to mark the site.

Legends apart, it is certain that Hearts got their name from the old jail, with Sir Walter Scott's novel *The Heart of Midlothian* having done much to popularise the romantic moniker. "It is a proud name and a graceful one," Mackie enthused, "even if it did at one time adorn a fetid prison, and it has demanded in its players a standard of football and of conduct in keeping with its grand sound. Even in its colloquial form 'Hearts' (pronounced in Edinburgh, as often as not, 'The Herts'), it speaks of affection around and within the team, and courage in the field of play."

Quite what Tom Purdie, the team's first captain, would have made of the nickname, "The Jam Tarts," coined from rhyming slang in the 1970s, is hard to say. Mark you, perhaps he would have felt it entirely in keeping with the mood of the times.

At any rate, the founding of Hibernian in 1875 and the move to Tynecastle in 1881 were easily the most important dates in Hearts' early history, marking the emergence of their local rivals and what was to be the club's home for more than a century. The first time Hearts met Hibs in the final of the Edinburgh Association Cup was on 9 February 1878. The match was played at Mayfield before 1,000 or so spectators. The *Scotsman* reporter of the day referred to Hearts as "the Heart" and summed up a goalless draw by opining that "the Hearts forwards did not seem to be altogether in trim, but the Hibernians played exceedingly well."

The replay also ended in a draw with Hibs grabbing a late equaliser that prompted "a scene of the wildest enthusiasm, the Irishmen tossing their hats, and jumping and cheering for several minutes while the players were mobbed by their enthusiastic partisans". Hearts took issue with Hibs' equaliser and refused to play extra time. Thus a third match was set for the end of February when admission prices were raised to encourage a more "select" class of spectator. Once more the game finished level, though the crowd was no less boisterous with a break-in of 800 spectators taking place after a second-half goal. The fourth attempt to settle the rivalry between the clubs endured the wrath of the *Scotsman* critic, who criticised Hearts and Hibs for "heavy and unnecessary charging, rash back kicking and an almost total want of dribbling and passing completely spoiling the beauties of the game."

What with hooliganism off the field and rough play on it, it seems some things have changed little in the course of one hundred years or so of derby matches. At any rate the fifth and final match of the series was a charity game with the proceeds of £13 going to Edinburgh's Royal Infirmary. Hearts won an exciting contest 3-2, though their winning goal was hotly disputed. (Again, it was ever thus.) The Edinburgh Cup was secured after a marathon battle and each Hearts player was given a Maltese Cross to note the victory. *The Scottish Football Annual* also took a dim view of these early derbies with the verdict that play was poor and "almost savage in the roughness."

During the 19th century Hearts won the Scottish Cup in 1891, beating Dumbarton. The Scottish League championship was taken in 1895 and 1897. Hearts won a ten-club league by five points from Celtic in their first championship success thanks to a run of 11 games without defeat. Leith Athletic and St Bernards were among the Edinburgh clubs that have since departed the scene. Two seasons later Hearts pipped Hibs for the title by two points after a dramatic last lap in the title race with a derby victory at Tynecastle the crucial difference between the sides. And in 1896 at Logie Green near Powderhall, in front of a 16,000 crowd, Hearts defeated Hibs 3-1 in the Scottish Cup final. This was a time of sweeping change both in terms of the rules and organisation of the game of association football. The penalty kick was introduced in 1890, goal nets in 1892, and professionalism reached the Scottish game in 1893. The involvement of the courts, which many thought was peculiar to the 1980s, stretches back as far as the 1890s when Renton, whom Hibs had defeated in the semi-final of the Scottish Cup, sought an interim interdict to stop the only Scottish Cup final ever to take place outside Glasgow going ahead. But Lord Low ruled that the game could take place, and goals from Baird, King and Michael proved decisive for Hearts on the day.

At the start of the 20th century Hearts won the Scottish Cup of 1901, defeating Celtic 4-3 in a famous final. The match took place at Ibrox before a relatively small crowd of 12,000. Conditions were stormy and Hearts were praised for using the right long-ball tactics while Celtic's short-passing game was unsuited to the circumstances. During this era Hearts were blessed with the talent of Bobby Walker, whose all-round ability made him the best inside-forward in Europe. Walker has always been a lucky name for Hearts and he was still involved in the first team when the Edinburgh club defeated Third Lanark in the 1906 Scottish Cup final. Walker was a Scotland regular for 13 years, winning 29 caps and playing 11 times against England. He was the first Hearts player to score 100 League goals, and one of the great personalities in the game before the First World War. Walker was such a valuable player to Hearts that when he failed to turn up for a match in 1909, the board refused to ratify a suspension imposed by manager James McGhee, who resigned on a point of principle.

Although the prizes were thin on the ground for long stretches of the century, Hearts were always strong on personality players. Paddy Crossan was a robust full-back in the 1920s who was wounded at the Battle of the Somme and died at the early age of 39 because of his wartime experiences. Andy Black had a reputation as an entertainer as well as a goalscorer in the 1930s. The trend of English players coming north encouraged in recent times by Rangers was anticipated at the turn of the century when Hearts brought Percy Dawson to Tynecastle from North Shields. The Geordie was Hearts' top scorer for three seasons and commanded a record British transfer fee when he moved to Blackburn Rovers in 1914. Jack Harkness was Hearts' most-capped goalkeeper, playing in the 1928 Wembley Wizards team that thrashed England 5-1. Barney Battles, born in Fisherrow but brought up in Boston, was an awesome physical specimen who scored on his debut in 1928, was regularly the club's top scorer and established a record of 44 League goals in a season which still stands today. Andy Anderson was one of the great Hearts international full-backs in the 1930s but, like so many others in the Tynecastle hall of fame, there were no medals to show for 475 matches of outstanding service.

In common with those already mentioned, Tommy Walker, who joined the Tynecastle ground staff in 1932, gained few winners' medals from an illustrious career with Hearts and Chelsea. The inside-forward was possibly the greatest midfield playmaker of his generation, and won the first of his twenty full international caps at the age of 19. Indeed, as a teenager involved in the Scotland v England match at Wembley, he took part in one of the most famous incidents in the history of the fixture. A penalty was awarded to Scotland. Walker was asked to take it. He placed the ball three times and three times the wind swirled it away. As the tension in the crowd grew, the cool Walker stroked the ball past the English goalkeeper to give Scotland an unforgettable victory.

After two years with Chelsea, Walker rejoined Hearts as assistant manager to Dave McLean. It was McLean who signed all three of the terrible trio – Alfie Conn, Willie Bauld and Jimmy Wardhaugh – for the trifling sum of £200. Walker took over as manager in his own right in 1951 and Hearts went on to enjoy the most successful period in the club's history.

After only three years of Tommy Walker's tenure as manager Hearts had made a breakthrough by winning the League Cup on 23 October 1954 at Hampden. Hearts had qualified from a section that included Celtic, Falkirk and Dundee. St Johnstone were beaten in the quarter-finals and Airdrie in the semi-finals; Against Motherwell in the national stadium Hearts won 4-2 with this team: Duff, Parker, Mackenzie, Mackay, Glidden, Cumming, Souness, Conn, Bauld, Wardhaugh, Urquhart.

The final was a personal triumph for Willie Bauld, who scored a hat-trick and confirmed his reputation as the "King of Hearts". Bauld was born in Newcraighall, an Edinburgh mining community, and played his early football with Musselburgh Union and Musselburgh Athletic. A brickmaker's apprentice, Bauld turned down the chance of a move to Sunderland and signed for Hearts in 1946, spending two years either on loan or playing junior football with Newtongrange and Edinburgh City to gain experience before playing in the first team. The ploy seemed to work since on his debut against East Fife, in the autumn of 1948, Bauld scored a hat-trick. For good measure, just in case anyone hadn't got the message first time round, he repeated the feat against Queen of the South the week after.

A handsome, fair-headed man with a deceptively casual style, Bauld was a maker as well as a taker of goals. He had a habit of coming deep and making late runs into the penalty box that was decades ahead of the fashion. His power in the air was legendary. Although he was only five feet eight inches tall, Bauld had the knack of seeming to freeze a moment in time, so remarkable was his talent of hanging in the air. Whatever the company Bauld, with his 356 goals for Hearts in just over 500 matches, would have been a candidate for immortality.

But in the company of Jimmy Wardhaugh and Alfie Conn – the terrible trio played for the first time together in that 6-1 win over East Fife – Bauld helped Hearts to haul in the silverware as well as earn the rave notices. Conn, Bauld and Wardhaugh all brought their own individual touch to the play of the Hearts forward line, but it was their collective excellence that Tommy Walker reckoned set them apart. "They always appeared to play as one. Their individual skills, expertise, positional sense and scoring ability were simply dovetailed into one unit," he said.

Wardhaugh was born near Berwick but moved to Edinburgh as a boy where he played for Shaftesbury Park Juveniles. It was after captaining the British A.T.C. in Geneva that Wardhaugh signed for Hearts in 1946. A clever user of the ball as well as a prolific goalscorer, Wardhaugh notched 375 goals for the club – a record that is unlikely ever to be matched.

Alfie Conn, a Prestonpans lad who provided the link between attack and defence, was particularly noted for his shooting power. A signing in 1944 from the juvenile ranks, it wasn't until the arrival of Bauld and Wardhaugh that Conn flourished. He scored 219 goals for Hearts. Between them the terrible trio contributed a phenomenal total of 950 goals to the club. It was a time when Hearts' firepower was so massive that winning games by ten goals or more was not the rarity it is today.

In 1956 Hearts took the first step towards a Scottish Cup success with wins over Forfar, Stirling, Rangers and Raith Rovers. The final against Celtic drew a crowd of 132,840 spectators to Hampden. Even though Hearts had not won the Cup for 50 years they went to the national stadium as favourites, the goals from Conn, Crawford and Bauld (2) that had eliminated Rangers having established their credentials.

If there was no doubt about Hearts' ability, it remained to be seen how they handled the big occasion against a team of Celtic's calibre. In fact Celtic were without their captain Stein as well as Collins, and a surprise team selection was kept from the Celtic players until just before kick-off time. Even without Bobby Parker, Hearts were good winners –

a point underlined by Tom Campbell and Pat Woods in their history of Celtic, *The Glory And The Dream*. According to the chroniclers of a hundred years of Celtic, "Hearts fully deserved their 3-1 win, and perhaps their greatest victory was over themselves and the burden of their reputation. Crawford was the danger man and scored twice; the first came after 21 minutes, a crisply hit shot from the edge of the penalty area. But the second only three minutes into the second half finished Celtic, a trundling half-hit shot from close range after Bauld had been allowed to meander unchallenged down the left wing. John Cumming epitomised the spirit of Hearts and their new sense of purpose by playing on with blood seeping through a bandage that barely covered a head wound. For once in a Scottish Cup final Celtic had been the other team."

Later to become the trainer in the course of a 26-year association with the club, John Cumming was a former miner who joined Hearts in 1950 from Carluke Rovers. He was known as the "iron man" and his contribution to the 1956 final was typical of a fearless individual.

D. MacLeod (Assistant Trainer), R. Kirk, D. Mackay, T. Mackenzie, T. Walker (Manager), W. Duff, W. Bauld, J. Cumming, J. Harvey (Trainer), A. Young, A. Conn, F. Glidden (Captain), J. Wardhaugh, J. Crawford.

The skill of the terrible trio and the grit of Cumming found a synthesis in the play of Dave Mackay, perhaps the finest-ever midfield player to wear a Hearts jersey. Mackay, who found success in England with Spurs and Derby, joined the club from Newtongrange Star in 1952 and his qualities of leadership were important features in the cup wins of 1954 and 1956. And when Hearts at last made the championship breakthrough during the 1957/58 season, it was Mackay's captaincy that inspired a team of stars.

Apart from the players already mentioned, Alex Young, who was to win Cup and League medals south of the border with Everton, contributed 24 goals and was the only player to play in every League match. Jimmy Murray scored 27 goals in 33 games, and there were also contributions from Andy Bowman, Ian Crawford, Bobby Blackwood and Johnny Hamilton. Hearts struck a record number of 132 championship goals, hitting nine against East Fife and Falkirk, eight against Queen's Park and seven against Third Lanark. Hearts claimed 62 points from 34 matches and won the title by 13 points from Rangers. Hearts scored five goals or more no fewer than nine times and their only defeat was against Clyde.

Hearts' reputation as Scotland's best team was underlined in the October of 1958 when they took the League Cup again, beating Partick Thistle at Hampden before a crowd of just under 60,000. Willie Bauld with two, Jimmy Murray with two and Johnny Hamilton were the scorers in a game where John Cumming was regarded by many as the man of the match.

The following autumn Hearts retained the League Cup, beating Third Lanark 2-1 before a 58,000 crowd at Hampden, thanks to goals from Johnny Hamilton and Alex Young. The big event of the 1959/60 season from the Tynecastle club's angle, though, was the winning of the championship. The previous year Hearts had been pipped for the title by Rangers after losing on the last day to Celtic. There were to be no slip-ups this time as Hearts again went through the 100-goal barrier and finished four points ahead of Kilmarnock. Tommy Walker, who had taken the team to their sixth major honour in his time as manager, put the success of the campaign down to "a full season of consistency." Hearts only used 16 players that year: Marshall, Kirk, Thomson, Cumming, Milne, Higgins, Smith, Young, Bauld, McFadzean, Crawford, Bowman, Murray, Brown, Blackwood and Hamilton.

Gordon Smith's transfer from Hibs was one of the big talking-points of a memorable season. When he made his debut for Hearts' second team, there were 12,000 spectators at Tynecastle to watch a reserve match. Afterwards the winger had to be smuggled out of the ground to avoid an army of autograph hunters. In Stewart Brown's book *Hibernian Greats*, Smith tells the story of how Hearts missed out on his signature as a youngster, but even in the twilight of his career Smith was able to play his part in a famous championship success. Bobby Parker recalls that Hearts' fame spread south of the border as well as north, and the Edinburgh club was regularly invited to play in games to mark the opening of floodlights at venues from Newcastle to Portsmouth.

After losing the League Cup final of 1961 to Rangers, Hearts won their seventh and last trophy of the Walker era, against Kilmarnock in October 1962. The difference between the teams was that Kilmarnock were without their playmaker, Sneddon, while Willie Hamilton, that most gifted of midfield players, was in top form for Hearts. Sandy Jardine, Hearts' co-manager, crossed swords with Hamilton during his time as a Rangers player, and while there were question marks against Hamilton's athleticism, Jardine recalled: "I think the sky would have been the limit for Willie Hamilton if his physical preparation had ever matched his skill level. Willie was a character, the type who'd turn up for a match abroad with one shirt in his bag, and maybe they don't make them like that any more."

A native of Airdrie, Hamilton played for Sheffield United and Middlesbrough before joining Hearts in the summer of 1962. It was from a brilliantly incisive run that Hamilton fashioned the goal for Norrie Davidson that won the final against Kilmarnock. Because of disciplinary problems, Hamilton was allowed to leave the club the following year. He played with Hibs and Aston Villa before spending another two years at Tynecastle after returning north in 1967. Hamilton was only 37 when he died after emigrating to Canada.

Hearts never finished lower than fourth in the League between 1950 and 1960. The next couple of decades were not anything like as consistently successful, though the 1965 vintage, with players of the calibre of Jim Cruickshank, an international goalkeeper, Willie Wallace, a striker who was to become part of the Lisbon Lions, Alan Anderson, Davie Holt, Willie Polland, Billy Higgins and Johnny Hamilton, didn't lack character. Having begun the season with an 8-1 win over Airdrie, it was ironic that Hearts should lose the last match of the campaign at home to Kilmarnock and forfeit the title on goal average. Hearts would have won on goal difference, but Kilmarnock's average of 1.88 pipped the Edinburgh side's 1.84 average.

The loss had a profound effect on Hearts and their supporters. The optimism that had been built up through the early 1950s and early

1960s was blown away by a new mood of despondency. A dark cloud settled over Tynecastle that would take almost 20 years to dispel.

Tommy Walker, who had been the club's manager for over 15 years, resigned in the autumn of 1966, and was succeeded, in spite of Parker's warnings, by the club coach, Johnny Harvey. Bobby Seith, a former Scottish youth coach, followed four years later. But the struggle showed no sign of relenting and John Hagart, an enthusiastic second-in-command, was entrusted with the job of reviving the club in the Premier Division. The last years saw the club suffer the indignity of relegation from the top ten in 1977 and Hagart was replaced by the former Scotland manager, Willie Ormond. The Musselburgh man's best days were behind him by this point in his career, and not until Bobby Moncur's appointment in 1980 did Hearts begin to see the wood for the trees. The former Newcastle player brought youngsters of the calibre of John Robertson, Gary Mackay and Dave Bowman to Tynecastle and sowed some of the seeds that would reap a benefit for the club in the 1980s.

Hearts have a tradition of great players. Here helping to launch a quiz book were (back row) Bobby Parker, Gordon Marshall and Walter Kidd. (Front Row) Alec Young, Johnny Hamilton, Gary Mackay and Donald Ford.

CHAPTER FOUR

Takeover

MIKE AITKEN

W ALLACE MERCER had always held an interest in sport. As a young man he'd played rugby for London Scottish. His first love in football was Glasgow Rangers and there was a time when he owned shares in the Ibrox club. As a successful businessman living and working in Edinburgh, Scotland's capital city, Mercer began to develop an affection for Hearts. At the beginning of the 1980s he was dismayed by the club's seemingly inexorable decline and followed with interest the attempt by the board of the day to change the club's constitution and open the door for the cash injection Hearts needed in order to survive.

Although he was grateful to Hearts for rekindling his love of football, Mercer had given no more serious thought to becoming involved in the running of a football club than he had to chartering a flight to the moon. At the time, saving Hearts from oblivion was probably the trickier task anyway. And, as a business venture, it made little economic sense to a man in his 30s, who had bought £1,000 worth of Hearts shares as a gesture of goodwill rather than through any ambition to get his foot in the door at Tynecastle.

When Donald Ford, one of the club's few players of distinction in the 1970s and a respected accountant outwith football, rang Mercer and asked him to join forces with the consortium attempting to beat off the bid of Edinburgh bookmaker and publican Kenny Waugh for control of Hearts, he was a little surprised at his own willingness to consider getting involved.

"I'd been watching Hearts for a few years and was very saddened by what I saw," Mercer recalls. "My wife Anne and I had bought some shares just as a gesture. We knew that Hearts were hitting the skids and that the club's bank had made this statement to the effect that unless they had a flotation to raise a substantial amount through £1 shares then the club could be closed."

Mercer would not care to present himself today as a knight on a gleaming white horse who came to the rescue of a fair club in distress. But Hearts were in a predicament and there was popular support that the club should not fall into the hands of just one man, however benevolent that dictatorship might be. The point of view of the shareholders' consortium was expressed by John Bell, an Edinburgh blacksmith, who told reporters that he supported only two teams — Hearts and Hearts reserves — and that his father had brought him to see Bobby Walker play. A traditionalist who wanted Hearts preserved as a social institution, Bell struck a folksy chord when he asked: "We have a Hearts war memorial down there at Haymarket. What would happen to that if something happened to this club?"

Wallace and Anne Mercer were considering making a financial contribution to Hearts and it was Anne who attended a shareholders' meeting in May 1981 when Wallace was in London entertaining business clients prior to watching the England v Scotland match at Wembley. The shareholders, encouraged by the then chairman, Archie Martin, agreed to open up the club through the release of 350,000 £1 shares.

Hearts had just had one of their worst-ever seasons — attendances for the entire year only totalled 120,000 — and the club was caught up in the vicious circle of low income and bad sales. The board of directors were to all intents and purposes a committee of trustees with little or no financial clout. Martin had tried hard to raise cash but appreciated that a major change was required in order to save Hearts from the gallows. Tinkering with the system wasn't going to alter anything. The shareholders eventually agreed and, once the club was opened up, Mercer, whose business activities in Edinburgh were flourishing, decided to put something back into the community to furnish the consortium with a contribution of around £30,000.

"The last thing on my mind," Mercer says, "was to get involved in the ego trip of buying, running or managing a football club. Apart from anything else, I didn't have any experience in football whatsoever. And at that stage I foolishly held the view that other people were bound to be better at it than me."

When Kenny Waugh, later to become chairman of Hibs for a number of years, made his bid for control of Hearts with the offer of a cheque for £255,000 – Waugh was friendly with Archie Martin – there was a feeling of panic amongst many interested parties who had the good of the club at heart that the directors would snap at the first offer that was made to them.

At this stage Ford telephoned Mercer at the Royal Garden Hotel. "He said to me, 'Look, we're in trouble. We need a saviour'. My first reaction was how on earth could I be a saviour? For a start, the kind of money that Hearts required had already been allocated in my plans for something else. Anyway, I rang one or two of my business clients that day, thought about the whole situation in the evening and spoke to my wife. She thought I was mad even to consider it. The next day I went to Wembley to see the England v Scotland game. That proved fatal. I enjoyed it, got caught up in the whole emotional thing, and went to Trafalgar Square in the evening. By this time I'd already been in touch with Archie Martin and told him that I was interested in competing with Kenny Waugh. I had to make a final decision that weekend, and getting involved in the whole euphoria of Wembley led me to take what I suppose was the not very sensible step of bidding for Hearts."

If, for once, Wallace Mercer's heart had ruled his business head, events subsequently began to gather a staggering momentum as the whole scenario unfolded under the starkest glare of publicity imaginable. Hearts might not have made many headlines for their prowess as a football team, but the battle for power in the boardroom attracted enormous interest, with frequent front-page news stories in the *Scotsman, Evening News* and *Glasgow Herald* supplementing the coverage on the sports pages.

On Monday, 25 May, a meeting was set up between Mercer and Archie Martin, Bert McKim and Iain Watt. The other directors, Bobby Parker and Alex Naylor, were absent. It was the first time Mercer had been through the front door at Tynecastle, and his abiding memory of the experience was noting that the then assistant manager, Tony Ford, was employed in giving a lick of paint to the home dressing-room.

Mercer was accompanied by his lawyer at the 9.30 a.m. meeting, where he bluntly told the directors that it had taken them ten years to get the club into its present state through mismanagement and various other factors. He advised them that they deserved the chance to consider their position for a few days. At this point Mercer was as much concerned with providing breathing-space for Hearts as anything else. At the end of the meeting he volunteered to put down a cheque for

£265,000. The invitation to the party had been delivered. Mercer appreciated that it was no longer a question of putting up a helpful contribution of £30,000. In order to compete with Kenny Waugh's bid he knew he had to be in it "for big ones".

A property developer, Mercer owned the Tynecastle sports and social club in Gorgie Road, Edinburgh. That evening he attended a meeting of the shareholders for the first time. "I hadn't met them before and they hadn't met me. At that stage they were running around like headless chickens because Kenny Waugh's bid was in and there was a lot of speculation about my involvement. I had words with them and they decided to jointly throw their hat into the ring with me. There were something like 150 shareholders there that night and I assured them that I didn't want to own Hearts for the sake of owning it," said Mercer.

Given this commitment, the consortium, including men like Alex Knight, Allan West and Bob Haig, came up with £85,000 from their own resources. This amount – and the consortium were prepared to go higher – effectively covered all the shares in the £350,000 issue.

The following day Mercer and the consortium presented the Hearts board with a cheque for £350,000 that seemed certain to guarantee them outright victory. But within an hour Kenny Waugh, who had set a deadline on his original bid of £255,000, tore up that cheque and presented a new one for £350,000. This time it was Waugh who told the media that he'd been approached by an interested group of shareholders to continue his stand against Mercer and the consortium.

The battle for Hearts was being conducted like a larger-than-life version of *The Price Is Right*, with both sides determined to come on down at the big finish. Chairman Archie Martin, who found himself in the Leslie Crowther role, decided that enough was enough and set a deadline of the following Wednesday, 3 June, by which time the identity of the winning contestant would be revealed. Martin said he was delighted with the number of people who had come forward and the depth of feeling shown for the club. "The players can sleep easy when they see the future of the club assured," he said. Martin also said that he wanted things to be done in the best interests of the club and not Archie Martin. Those proved to be prophetic words, for Martin was not to survive the boardroom upheaval of the following week. But his contribution to setting up the share issue was vital to allowing a wind of change to blow through Tynecastle.

At any rate, the days leading up to the announcement of the board's decision turned out to be more like a presidential election than anything

My first visit in 1981 through the front door at Tynecastle.

else. Mercer appeared to blast the winning strike when he talked of a possible sponsorship deal with Skol that was entirely dependent on the bid by Pentland (Mercer's firm) being successful. Waugh responded by disclosing that he had the support of Ronnie Watt and the Hearts shareholders' association. "Mercer has put forward proposals but nothing concrete. I am the only one to have put my cheque on the table. Let's see Mercer put his on the table," Waugh told the *Scotsman*. Mercer responded to that challenge by stating that he had assets of £2.5 million and that there were plans for a £500,000 recreation and training complex at Tynecastle if the consortium were successful.

Most of Edinburgh and a large section of the Scottish public were riveted by this battle for power that had been allowed to unfold in the very best traditions of the glitzier soap operas. Tom Watson of the Hearts supporters' federation was for Mercer, Sheriff Archie Bell was for Waugh. Outside the boardroom there was a split of opinion and inside Tynecastle the decision of Hearts' five-man board promised to be equally close.

It was Mercer, though, who was established as the candidate with the higher profile. The night before the directors met to choose between Waugh and Mercer, Mercer invited fans to the supporters' club premises in Slateford for an evening of information and entertainment. An advertisement in the *Evening News* also promised some favourite ex-players and the presence of Allan Wells. Looking back on that night, Mercer remembers: "That was my first-ever public performance. I've had a few since, but that was the night I sat on the stage of the Hearts supporters' club and answered questions for an hour in response to anyone who had anything to ask. The meeting was chaired by Donald Ford and I came in from the back of the hall. One newspaper said that I entered like a presidential candidate. But it was a purely intuitive thing, not stage-managed at all. I didn't have a public relations consultant then and I still don't have one now. It was just natural showmanship, for what it was worth."

There were those who hoped that Mercer and Waugh would get together and run the club jointly, but that was never a realistic possibility on either side, even though Archie Martin thought that it was a tragedy. With two more or less identical offers to consider the Hearts board had to make a straightforward decision. "What we must do is establish whose personality is best suited to Hearts," Martin said before a meeting that was to effectively end his 20-month involvement with Hearts as a catalyst of change. "We've had to swallow our pride and admit that things were bad. Now, whoever wins will ensure that Hearts have the basic foundations of the club right for the future."

Going into the decisive board meeting, Mercer knew that he could count on the votes of Alex Naylor and Iain Watt. Archie Martin and Bert McKim were for Waugh. That left the vote of Bobby Parker, the former chairman, as decisive. Extraordinary as it may seem, Parker had been on holiday in Majorca throughout this crucial period in the club's history and was uncontactable for days. Parker, a former player with the club and still a director today, threw his hat in with Mercer and his vote eventually won the day on a 3-2 majority. Before then, however, there had been a final twist in the tail when the directors had insisted that Mercer put his cheque for £265,000 on the table. Mercer did eventually present the cheque but found the circumstances distasteful. "In business matters you put in a lawyer's letter – and that means the offer is binding and you're committed. You don't usually have to walk in with a cheque. That morning I got in touch with the National Westminster Bank, who came back to me in ten minutes and said, 'Yes, you can write a cheque for the down-payment of £265,000'. I walked into the Hearts boardroom half-an-hour before they were due to meet and said to them: 'Gentlemen, if that's the way you do business, there's my cheque', and I threw it on the table."

Having won the vote 3-2, Mercer heard the news sitting in the Tynecastle Arms, and a secret meeting was set up for later that evening between Mercer and Martin in the Caledonian Hotel. "He told me that all along he thought I'd be a good guy and that he wanted to stay on the board. I told him that his fellow directors would make a decision on that when we met the next day," recalled Mercer.

Before then, there was a Press conference at Tynecastle to hail the new "King" or "Ace" of Hearts, depending on which tabloid newspaper you read. In seven years as chairman of Hearts, Mercer was to develop an unrivalled grasp of the media's needs, but he's never forgotten that first encounter: "Never in my life have I had a Press conference like it, nor will it ever happen again. There were photographers and television cameramen falling over themselves. It was tremendous stuff and suddenly I realised that I'd inherited control of Hearts."

From the moment Donald Ford had telephoned him in London up until the 11 a.m. Press conference when the then 34-year-old Mercer assumed control took only twelve days. Even by Mercer's own standards, it was a whirlwind entrepreneurial ride.

Of course, the last thing the new man in charge was likely to do was let sleeping dogs lie. Before lunch, Bert McKim, the general manager of a bank in Edinburgh, had tendered his resignation as a director, on a point of honour. In later years McKim was to write to Mercer, conceding that he'd made a mistake, and that if he'd known Mercer at the time he would have voted differently. Martin wanted to stay on, but given his support for Waugh there was never much chance of him surviving. "I was at my first board meeting, and rather than get involved in the debate, I left it with the other directors to talk to Archie privately. I went through to the secretary's office, and five minutes later he came through to tell me that he was resigning," Mercer remembers. Whatever the differences between Mercer and Martin at the time, six years later the pair were on more cordial terms. Martin contacted Mercer in 1987 to tell him that he'd been good news for the club, and sold the chairman his shares.

It was ironic that the man that Martin replaced as chairman, Bobby Parker, should eventually outlast the young lion. Parker, indeed, is the only surviving director from the pre-Mercer era largely because his knowledge of football and link with the great Hearts side of the 1950s provides a significant connection between the club's present and its past. Parker, however, was too tainted with the failure of previous Tynecastle administrations to re-inherit the title of chairman when Mercer decided that he lacked the experience to assume the mantle that was his right as the majority shareholder. Instead, Alex Naylor, an Edinburgh publican, became Hearts' third chairman in little more than a year.

Mercer had pressed Naylor into service because he felt he didn't know enough about football. But in every important aspect Mercer felt he was running the club from the word go. "I was the majority shareholder and every decision from that first board meeting was mine," he said. "And, without wishing to sound arrogant, every idea the club has put forward since was also mine. I would say that I have now gathered a team round about me and I will support their decisions. But from the minute I walked into that first board meeting the man in charge of Hearts has effectively been Wallace Mercer."

If that was obvious to all and sundry, nevertheless one of the planks of Mercer's campaign against Waugh was that he did not want total control. "In due deference to the chairmanship of the Heart of Midlothian football club, I truly felt that you shouldn't just buy it. I felt that I needed to serve my apprenticeship on the board. If you like, I'd been flung from the back-benches into the cabinet. At that point I didn't feel I was quite ready for the Prime Minister's job," he said.

The partnership with Naylor was to last less than a year as the club's financial problems intensified and Naylor decided that enough was enough. But the man whose only previous contact with the Scottish football establishment was in Glasgow as the one-time Rangers' manager, Scot Symon's milk boy was about to prove that he was no quitter.

When I first took control of Hearts I didn't think it was right to assume the chairmanship and Alex Naylor filled the role for a spell.

CHAPTER FIVE

Turned Down by McLean and Wallace

MIKE AITKEN

THE ARRIVAL of Wallace Mercer as Hearts' majority shareholder did not bring an instant cure to a patient that had been sick for ten years. The new man in charge decided to gamble on a policy of recruitment in a bid to administer some comfort to the invalid – but it was a slow process and things were to get worse before they got better.

In retrospect, Mercer assesses his first year at Tynecastle as a learning experience. To some extent he was making it up as he went along, and what was clear from the outset was that the new broom would not retain many vestiges of the old order. Archie Martin had gone, much to the consternation of the shareholders' consortium, and it was only a matter of time before manager Bobby Moncur – a friend as well as an associate of Martin's – was also on his way. A Press conference was held that both Moncur and Mercer attended in a bid to paper over the cracks. At the time I reported that they didn't quite manage to carry off the image of a Morecambe and Wise or a Hope and Crosby. Just thirteen days later Moncur quit.

Whatever was said publicly at the time, Moncur and Mercer didn't hit it off. "Bobby Moncur obviously had the back door open before I walked in the front," Mercer recollected. "We only lasted a for a few days. I didn't like the cut of his jib and I was delighted when he resigned. In fact, at the first board meeting I attended at Tynecastle with Alex Naylor, I had to order Moncur to sit with the chairman. He refused to break bread with Naylor. I said if you don't, you're out. In the end, Moncur decided to leave within a few days."

When Hearts secured Moncur's services from Carlisle they had to pay the English club £30,000 in compensation. It was the measure of the more businesslike approach Mercer was to bring to Hearts' affairs that he demanded compensation from Moncur to release the manager from his contract. "My first bit of business was to get Moncur to pay us to leave – I think the cheque was for around £13,000 – and that was the beginning of the new era," Mercer said.

Bobby Moncur and I didn't get along and he soon quit as manager of Hearts.

Bobby Moncur had taken over as manager of Plymouth Argyle within a matter of days and Hearts were on the lookout for their fifth manager in seven years (Bobby Seith, John Hagart and Willie Ormond were the others). Although the details were kept under wraps at the time, Hearts were prepared to think big as Mercer began to reshape the organisation. "I might not have known all that much about football, but what I did know was that I thought that the Hearts team that had gone down were not capable mentally of lifting themselves up to win promotion. The team had to be torn apart – it was a ruthless task, both on and off the field," said Mercer.

As Willie Gibson went out the door to Partick Thistle for £30,000, Derek Strickland, a former Rangers player, arrived from Leicester, and moves were set in motion to secure a power player, after the disappointment at missing out on Willie Garner, who preferred to join Celtic when he left Aberdeen.

Without a replacement for Bobby Moncur – Tony Ford was in charge of the first team – Mercer was left to act in the transfer market. "I signed my first hard man within a week. Stuart McLaren came to us from Dundee after helping them into the Premier Division. He'd been over the course before as captain with Motherwell. I didn't know anything about him as a player, but when he took a seat opposite me in the boardroom I noticed he had pale blue eyes and tight skin across the forehead. I thought he looked like a gunfighter." From day one, Mercer operated a policy that a new player either signed after discussions or he left. There was to be no halfway house. Mercer's assessment of McLaren as a man clinched the signature for £25,000.

If there were one or two new faces on the field of play, the manager's chair remained worryingly vacant. Alex Rennie and Willie McLean were among the men tipped for the post, but the two people Hearts had at the top of their shopping-list were Jock Wallace and Jim McLean.

The absence of a manager didn't stop the club trading in the transfer market. Roddie McDonald was signed from Celtic for £55,000 – at the time it was a record fee for Hearts – and his value to the club was keenly felt until he moved to Morton six years later. Gerry McCoy from Queen's Park and Pat Byrne, an Irish midfield player from Leicester, took Mercer's tally to five before a new man was installed as manager. Perhaps the most valuable signing of all, though, was the least heralded at the time. Goalkeeper Henry Smith was bought from Leeds United for £2,000. In 1988 he was the regular understudy to Jim Leighton as the Scotland goalkeeper.

Both Byrne and Strickland came from Leicester, where Jock Wallace was the manager at the time. Mercer would have liked nothing better than to offer the former Rangers manager and Tynecastle coach the opportunity to rebuild Hearts. "Jock rang me to tell me that we couldn't afford him," said Mercer. "He said he'd see me on the highways and byways. But he turned down our job offer."

Hearts had more than one managerial iron in the fire at this point, and when Jock Wallace said 'no', Mercer stepped up the chase for Jim McLean of Dundee United. "I never met him personally, but there were a few occasions when we spoke privately and, of course, we asked the Dundee United board for permission to approach their manager. Even when they turned us down, McLean said he might think about it at the end of the year."

Unable to secure a quality manager at the first time of asking, Hearts decided to entrust Englishman Tony Ford with the post. "He was only ever put in that position as a stop-gap appointment," said Mercer. "I had no intention of him lasting the course. In fact it was quite funny because, within ten days of getting the job, Tony began to believe his own publicity. He went from painting the dressing-room to being a superstar who wore the white jackets and drank the gins."

Even as a short-term measure, the decision to appoint Ford, whose knowledge of the Scottish scene was limited, backfired on Mercer. Hearts didn't make the expected progress and, far from hailing a new dawn, the Edinburgh *Evening News* said of the club that "hooliganism, dull soccer, poor skills and shoddy facilities have all contributed to empty grounds and lack of atmosphere".

Mercer said: "After the first two or three months of the 1982 season it was obvious that Hearts were not going to get promotion. I had gambled everything. In a personal sense, my house was on the line, I was short of cash in my business and I'd given the club an interest-free loan of £50,000. I'd also given Hearts a personal guarantee for £100,000 and another £25,000 loan. I was 35 years of age and within seven days of the takeover I was in for £500,000. It was money I had, but I also didn't have. So I slashed the overheads of running this blessed club, I got rid of three-quarters of the administrative staff; and, it would be fair to say, I cut everything back to the bone. I reduced the players' salaries and we went to a very thin system of low salaries and incentives. But after three months it was apparent that we weren't going to win promotion."

Ford, clearly, had to go. The question of turning the club around was broader, however, than just the identity of the next manager. "This was when I either made my classic mistake or *coup*, depending on how you looked at it," said Mercer. "Alex Naylor, the chairman, said I'd be a hero to the fans if we pulled it off. I rang up Jim McLean in Monte Carlo, where he'd taken Dundee United to play Monaco on UEFA Cup business. On the bench for United that night were Willie Pettigrew and Derek Addison. For £165,000 we signed those players – with so much up front and so much on the never-never. Tony Ford had promised me that we'd be able to sell Alex MacDonald either to Morton or St Mirren,

full-back Peter Shields would go for £40,000 and someone else would
also be moving on. In other words, I was told we'd be able to raise about
£80,000 towards the incoming deal so we could meet the balance.

"That was my fatal mistake, to believe what the manager said. In fact
we didn't sell any of those players. Alex MacDonald was having injury
problems at the time and we came within a hair's-breadth of trading him
to St Mirren in exchange for Lex Richardson plus quite big money. At
that time Alex MacDonald had been one of the less sensible buys for
Hearts football club in a financial sense, though that's not to criticise his
many talents as a player. He'd been bought from Rangers at the end of his
career by Archie Martin. They paid a huge signing-on fee, which was
fair enough since Alex didn't get a testimonial from Rangers. And there
was a fee of around £35,000. Now Alex was a tremendous professional,
but as a playing investment for the future he probably only had about
two years left. Hearts were not in a position to make crazy investments
like that. But what we did have was a player of enormous ability and
experience. Bobby Parker at that time was very impressed with Alex –
both as a person and as team captain. Bobby said to me: 'Wallace, we've
got our future manager on the staff already'. But the trouble was, it was
too early for Alex."

Mercer regarded Parker, who has served Hearts as a player, a coach
and in the boardroom as both chairman and director, as his mentor ever
since those early days. Instead of allowing Alex MacDonald to leave the
club, Mercer blocked the moves on an intuitive, gut feeling. There were
genuine worries after an aborted comeback against Queen's Park
whether or not MacDonald would be able to play again (in fact he was
back in action within three months), but Hearts had other plans in mind
for an outstanding player many regarded as undervalued during his
days at Ibrox.

Under Ford's stewardship Hearts had played cautiously and failed to
set the box office on fire at Tynecastle. "By this time I didn't have any
more money to spend on players and it struck me during a game against
Queen's Park that Ford would have to go. I went into the boardroom at
half-time and told the other directors. Their response was that I
couldn't do it. I repeated that Ford was going.

"I flirted that night with the idea of bringing Tommy Docherty to
Tynecastle. Fortunately, Alex Naylor put me off the idea by midnight.
On the Sunday morning I placed a call to Alex MacDonald's house and
Alex met me for lunch at the Royal Scot Hotel. I said to him, 'You're the
team captain – what do you think has gone wrong?' He gave me his ideas
on what we could do. I then asked him to do me a favour – I said if he

would handle the playing side, I'd deal with all the paper work. At that point there was no talk of Alex being the manager – the job was that of player-coach."

The signing of Willie Pettigrew from Dundee United was a financial millstone round the club's neck.

Mercer promised MacDonald his full backing and the opportunity to test the waters of management. The following morning, news of Ford's dismissal was announced and MacDonald took over. Although two of Britain's biggest and most powerful clubs – Liverpool with Kenny Dalglish and Rangers with Graeme Souness – subsequently appointed player-managers, Hearts' decision to make MacDonald a player-coach was a novel and innovative move that didn't meet with unqualified approval at the time. Even the late Jock Stein, who wasn't wrong about many things in the course of an illustrious career, questioned the wisdom of a full-time club asking a player to be manager.

Initially, Alex MacDonald was a little reluctant about expressing the ambition to become a manager. And, indeed, Hearts still harboured what were to be unfulfilled hopes that Jim McLean could be tempted to

take the manager's post with MacDonald as the number two. That
didn't work out, however, and since MacDonald was making a good
impression in the job, Hearts were happy to let the coach find his feet
without the pressure of the managerial tag. McLean had said he would
consider the Hearts offer when his contract was over, but Dundee
United pre-empted any move by making an improved deal that
November.

Events off the field continued to lead a merry dance as chairman Alex
Naylor became the next Hearts director to quit. "The chairman
resigned in January of 1982 because we couldn't pay our bills to Dundee
United," Mercer said. "One of Naylor's publicly expressed reasons for
resigning was that we were trying to sell David Bowman to the
Tannadice club. In fact it was Alex Naylor who tried to do that. For the
rest of that season no one was chairman of Hearts. In January we didn't
have a manager either, but in February we gave the job to Alex."

In retrospect, this was very much an act of faith on Mercer's part, for
the Scottish Cup defeat by Forfar was as ignominious a result in Hearts'
history as was Rangers' defeat by Berwick. The reaction of the late John
Fairgrieve in the *Sunday Mail* may not have been a balanced view, but
his call to turn Tynecastle into a car park certainly touched a chord
amongst the faithful.

What kept Mercer going through these dark days was the
understanding that he'd not only inherited three young players of
exceptional promise (Gary MacKay, John Robertson and David
Bowman), but also a sense of social obligation that was nowhere to be
found in the fine print of the balance sheet. "There was an enormous
emotional need for Hearts to do well," Mercer remembers. It was an
obligation he felt he couldn't shed lightly.

As it turned out, Hearts missed promotion that season and the
newspaper headlines all spoke of a deepening crisis. The 1-0 defeat at
home to Motherwell that condemned Hearts to their fourth season in
the First Division in six years was one of the least savoury afternoons in
an apparently unending catalogue of woe. The start was delayed by five
minutes to allow an unusually large crowd for the time of over 14,000
into the ground. With players of the calibre of Brian McClair and
Willie Irvine, Motherwell took the field as worthy First Division
champions. They were able to play like free spirits while a nervous
Hearts team never got over the loss of an early goal.

The disappointment on the field, however, was dwarfed by the
miserable events on the terracings when violence erupted during the
second half. Seven arrests were made and three policemen taken to

hospital for treatment. Wallace Mercer himself walked right into the front line to quell the trouble. "It was one of the most fateful days of my life," said Mercer, "What with the financial consequences of not winning promotion and the social cost of the riot. It was the climax of a first year in football that had shown me clearly what to do and what not to do. The experience was an enormous one. Some people in Scottish football turned around after a year and said, 'That man doesn't know what he's doing or talking about', but I probably learned more in twelve months about running a football club than 90 per cent of football club directors would ever know. The fact of the matter was that I was running the club as a business."

After a season of crushed hopes, it was time for Mercer to take stock. The dread of part-time football was in the air, and the problems

When crowd trouble flared in 1982 I went to the terraces to appeal for calm – and came away with a sense of the deep frustration felt by many Hearts' supporters.

experienced by Hearts were threatening to drag Mercer's private business interests into equally stormy waters. There could be no more hand-outs. Hearts had to become self-sufficient, and Mercer made it plain that from here on in the Tynecastle operation would stand on its merits. "Truthfully, I thought that my company was going to go down the tubes. I was under personal financial pressure because I'd lent money to the club that they couldn't give me back. Even my house was on the line – and Hearts hadn't made it," said Mercer.

Since taking over Hearts, Mercer had experienced a roller-coaster ride in which he freely admitted he didn't know where the next dip was coming from. The week after the 1981/82 season ended brought the chance to consider a more even-keeled journey into the future. Directors Iain Watt and Bob Haig were to depart the boardroom, while trainer Andy Stevenson was shed from the backroom staff. There was room for new blood and Mercer could at last pick his own team behind the scenes.

CHAPTER SIX

Out of the Maelstrom

MIKE AITKEN

A YEAR AND A DAY after becoming the owner of Hearts, Wallace Mercer gave up control. Ironically, on the day he sold 15 per cent of the club's stock to Douglas Park for £75,000, Mercer took over as chairman. Mercer's promotion (he still owned 43 per cent) plus the arrival of Park and Pilmar Smith on the board of directors in June 1982 was a turning-point for Hearts. The following month both the management and the playing side of the set-up would be enhanced by Sandy Jardine's move from Ibrox. A new team was running a club that had been saved by the bell.

Their arrival could hardly have been better timed. Given the problems facing a club that was £500,000 in debt and could not shake off the habit of life in the First Division, the appearance of the Fifth Cavalry at Tynecastle would not have gone amiss. According to the new chairman it was a last-chance season, for Hearts could not survive indefinitely as a full-time outfit outwith the Premier Division.

Mercer reckons he has had to make two very difficult decisions in the course of his association with Hearts. The first was the initial move to become involved at Tynecastle. The second was keeping faith with a full-time set-up after a year in which the club declared a loss of £382,873 and gate receipts only produced £144,000. Hearts' fans were not so much flooding as trickling through the turnstiles.

Pilmar Smith, an Edinburgh bookmaker and lifelong Hearts supporter, was given the job of improving relations between the club and its followers. He remarked: "In the past some directors here would not have known what a real supporter looked like. That had to end." By way of proving his point, Smith restored the photographs of the 1958 and 1962 trophy-winning teams to the manager's office. Hearts didn't plan to live in the past, but nor did they want to forget it.

While Douglas Park, a West of Scotland coach operator with no previous interest in Hearts, was asked to supervise the commercial aspect of the club's development (Park's role was not on a day-to-day basis but he broadened Hearts' horizons), Mercer began to envisage a sounder financial base for a club that was forbidden from entering the transfer market until their debts to Celtic, for Roddy McDonald, and Dundee United, for Willie Pettigrew and Derek Addison, were settled. "By not winning promotion, I thought at the time we had blown it and let everyone down," Mercer said. "On the day we were beaten by Motherwell I felt as if I was going to the guillotine in the sun. With the benefit of hindsight, of course, the extra year in the First Division was the best thing that ever happened to us; because without a period of apprenticeship, it gave me another year to learn my job and gave Alex another 12 months to learn his."

There was a basic formula Hearts tried to follow in a bid to make the club financially viable. Savings were made by selling players, the promotional and commercial sides were built up and promising young players like Gary Mackay, John Robertson and David Bowman were given their chance to make an impact. In addition, Jardine's arrival on a free transfer as assistant player-manager after 17 years with Rangers did much to boost morale. "Alex MacDonald had become the Hearts coach and was looking for someone to work with him," Jardine said. "He wanted me to come to Tynecastle, and I asked Rangers if they would give me a free transfer. I had to talk with John Greig and he agreed to let me go. Once Rangers had given the go-ahead there was a meeting between Wallace Mercer and myself at which everything was arranged. There was speculation that I might have gone to England, but once Hearts wanted me there was never any argument about where I would end up. I even took a cut in wages to join them."

As Jardine and MacDonald set about improving Hearts' fortunes on the field of play – "The team wasn't ready for the Premier Division and there was a lot of work to be done," said Jardine – Mercer had to deal with a gloomy financial situation off the field. Apart from Dundee United and Celtic, Hearts also owed money to the bank and Lothian and Borders police. "We had to seize the opportunity to recast the business," Mercer remembered. "But it was at this point I got myself into really stormy waters. I did something I will never do again and am ashamed of. At the time I did it out of desperation. I got Bobby Parker to sell Derek Addison to St Johnstone. The fee was £55,000, which was the sum we'd paid for him and represented a terrific bit of business from our point of view. It was a brilliant deal given the amount of pressure we were under from the bank. But rather than the money going to Dundee United to pay off the transfer, it went to the bank. As the prime creditor, they were putting the most pressure on us. We siphoned off a little money to bring Sandy Jardine to the club, but after his arrival the Scottish League pulled the shutters down on us and we couldn't go into the market again. So we were left with the remnants of the team that had failed to win promotion, and Jardine. In retrospect we got promotion that season more by grace and good fortune than anything else."

While Hearts' indebtedness to Dundee United won much publicity at the time – Mercer was furious with Jim Farry, the secretary of the Scottish League, for going public on the matter – a secret meeting took place at Tannadice between the two sides in a bid to sort out an embarrassing situation. "Dundee United were hounding us and Bobby Parker and I went up to Tannadice to attend a board meeting. I'd never

Rivals become colleagues – Gary Mackay, whom I almost sold to Dundee United in the early 1980s, and Eamonn Bannon who joined Hearts from United in 1988.

met their directors before. Jim McLean came in, and they wanted to know what we were going to do. I'll be quite honest and say that in order to get United off my back I offered to sell them Dave Bowman and Gary Mackay. But they were only prepared to offer £30,000 each for the players and we said 'no'. Bobby took me to the Swallow Hotel in Dundee and bought me lunch. Over a bottle of Niersteiner he told me that he was going to stick with me and see the thing through."

Keeping the experienced head of Parker in a changing team of directors, while adding the freshness of Pilmar Smith and Douglas Park to a boardroom in which Mercer assumed the chairman's seat for the first time, proved to be a winning formula. "We've not looked back since then," said Mercer, "because we've had the same team in the boardroom and the same team in the manager's office. We've all worked together and, effectively, Hearts have three managers – Alex MacDonald, Sandy Jardine and Wallace Mercer. That position has not changed since the summer of 1982."

While winning promotion from the First Division as runners-up to St Johnstone was achieved through hard work rather than flamboyance, off the field Mercer brought a touch of entrepreneurial sparkle to Tynecastle. The second leg of the League Cup semi-final between Hearts and Rangers in November 1982 was notable for the innovation of a lottery in which a £35,000 house and a new car were given away through programme sales. "If it was imagination and not goals that counts, Heart of Midlothian FC would be grinning atop the Premier Division," enthused a leader in the Edinburgh *Evening News*. "Their sparkling off-the-field play of providing a prize sponsorship deal with a £35,000 house and a new car . . . is a move of devastating brilliance. Shades of Conn, Bauld and Wardhaugh on the field."

In order to keep the wolf from the door, Hearts didn't go without help. "For example, the Miller Group gave me a house and Alexanders gave me a car," Mercer said. "As a First Division club we'd done well to reach the semi-finals of the League Cup. Robin Fry had joined us on the commercial side and Douglas Park and I got our heads together and came up with this idea to sell programmes, with the prize of a car and a house, in a bid to make some money and reduce what we owed to Dundee United. It caught everyone's imagination."

A former employee of Miller's, Mercer was grateful to his old company for their sponsorship and to Jock Stein for lending his authoritative presence to the occasion by making the draw. Challenge matches against quality European sides like Dynamo Kiev, the Soviet champions, special season-ticket deals and cheap buses for supporters to away ties were just some of the novel presentations to come out of the good ideas factory at Tynecastle during this period. "For two years I was like the White Tide man," Mercer said. "Everything was for sale. We were even the first First Division club in Scotland to have a shirt sponsor when Alexanders came in."

Scottish club football was at a low ebb in 1983. Hearts were not the only big name feeling the pinch. Other big city clubs were also toiling, and at a meeting held at Easter Road, the Hibernian ground, the late Chris Anderson, one of the game's most distinguished legislators, argued that "unless we act to heal the wounds, there are those who will face extinction". It was a theme Mercer was quick to echo and endorse. Whatever specific problems Hearts were facing, he knew that football in general had to come up with a plan for the future that made sense in business terms. The topic of reconstruction was to dominate Scottish football for a number of years, and although a breakaway was eventually resisted, Hearts played a forceful role in the case for change.

But before Mercer could take part in the debate to improve the Scottish scene, he had to help Hearts to get their act together first. "What we had to do was cut the professional staff back to just ten professionals. We didn't even have a physiotherapist. In the office there was just Les Porteous and a part-time secretary. And when the Scottish League eventually lifted their ban on us buying players we had to have a board meeting to decide whether or not we could afford to pay £2,000 for Malcolm Murray. We couldn't, so we agreed to pay £1,000 plus take part in a testimonial match in Buckie. I remember the entire Hearts board went along to Lesser Hampden to watch Malcolm Murray make his debut for the club in a reserve game as a trialist. It was a freezing cold night and we all had to make the decision as to whether the player was worth the money. It was hard to envisage a situation five years on where I would be able to sanction an investment of £600,000 in new players," he said.

The club that once relied on lotteries for houses, cars and holidays to break even is now one of the most successful operations in British football. "We've made profits five years out of six," said Mercer, "and I mean trading profits. The assets are also up from £400,000 to something like £6 million or £7 million. Today we operate on an overdraft of under £500,000. We've got a debt-to-assets ratio of one to ten, which is as good as any British business. The player pool is conservatively worth £2.5 million. Since I took over we've invested £1.8 million in new players – and only a few hundred thousand pounds of that have come from sales. As far as the stadium is concerned, we've spent £500,000 on improving Tynecastle. It is only in the past couple of years I've taken a nominal fee. But other than that the directors haven't taken a penny out of Hearts.

"It was apparent to us from the start that the only way we would get success was through good players. I felt it then, and it is even more clear to me now, that the game is about players. It is not about chairmen, or directors or managers. And my job was to get the people out there, the supporters, to come. The only way to keep them was through the players. I've stayed faithful to the supporters and given them a straight shake-down. One of the important things from my point of view after the first three years was that I was able to get my loans repaid. People in Scottish football forget – they think, oh, he was only just involved and he put his cash in. But I had to serve a two-year training period before we got to the Premier Division. It was a hard, hard road."

No one at Tynecastle needs much reminding of Hearts' humble position in 1982. "I took it for granted with Rangers that there was fresh training gear whenever I wanted it and that if I needed new boots all I had to do was ask. Those early days with Hearts were a rude awakening for me regarding life outside the top flight," said Sandy Jardine.

Having secured promotion from the First Division – it was no mean feat given that Hearts were big fish in a little pond and opposition teams raised their game in front of the big crowds attracted by the Edinburgh team – Hearts were immediately installed as favourites to go back down again.

After the Scottish League's ban on signing players was lifted, Hearts attempted to stay in the big time by signing experienced types for bargain prices – Willie Johnston, Jimmy Bone and Donald Park came into this category, joining up with the likes of Jardine, MacDonald and McLaren. Alex MacDonald's managerial philosophy was simple. "We weren't going to take any doings," he said. Not only did Hearts avoid heavy defeats in their first year back in the top ten, but they also played with enough spirit and style to secure a place in the following season's UEFA Cup. Here at last was a tangible sign of Hearts moving away from the "yo-yo" syndrome, the constant flitting between First and Premier Divisions that had threatened the very existence of the club.

While the players enjoyed a champagne celebration after the 1-1 draw with Celtic, Mercer was pitched fully clothed into the bath. He might have been soaked from head to toe, but there was a sunny grin for the cameras on his face as at last the investment made in the club began to make some kind of sense. Privately, however, it had been a harrowing time for the ebullient chairman.

International quartet – (from left) Henry Smith, John Colquhoun, Gary Mackay and Dave McPherson were all part of the Scotland squad that travelled to Malta.

"My involvement with Hearts had set back my business career by four years," said Mercer. "It meant that I had to go into partnership with the Life Association of Scotland. Due credit to them, they helped me to set up a property company, the Dunedin Group, which I now run very successfully for them and have a major interest in. But the only reason I was open to that offer was because I was under heavy financial pressure.

"I'd had a problem with an important business venture, interest rates were rising, the company was haemorrhaging heavy losses, and I was under enormous personal pressure.

"Even though I could see my business crumbling I was determined to hold on to my Hearts shares. I had a very tough three years. People don't know just how difficult things got on a personal level for me. At one stage I thought I was going to have a nervous breakdown.

"I had to keep my mind and body together, and the only way I survived that three-year period was by getting away for a week's holiday in America or somewhere like that. In some respects I was living the life of a schizophrenic – because, mentally, I was thinking about a move to the States. I suppose you could say I was planning an out if things ever got really sticky for my family and myself.

"The holidays were the only thing that kept me going. It is a lonely job being the number one. I was the front man at Tynecastle, I'd set up Dunedin, and there were all the problems at my other company, Pentland, which had got into storms of debt. Everything that I'd built up was in danger of being frittered away.

"All I had was my investment in Hearts, my home, my family and the beginning of a new project with Dunedin. After three years or so of weathering the storms, things began to get a little better. But it was only in the last couple of years, after having gone through that whole roller-coaster ride, that things came out on the right side. What I've got now is a situation where I'm a lot stronger personally. And my business is a slimmer operation as well as being much more valuable. I think I've come out of it all as a better businessman; more importantly, a better human being too.

"But during the bad times not even my directors at Tynecastle knew the financial pressure I was under. If it hadn't been for the help of a number of people I wouldn't be here today. There were two occasions, for instance, when Jim Souness, who played for Hearts during the 1950s when he was training to be an actuary, and now works for the Life Assurance of Scotland, gave me loans that eased the pressure at the bank. If they hadn't taken those decisions at that stage I would have gone under.

"I remember going to a fateful meeting in London with bankers where I was interviewed over lunch and had to sing for my supper. They rang me back to say they'd lend me the money that would give me the opportunity to have a year's breathing-space.

"At one stage I'd gone to San Francisco to get away from it all for a few days. I woke up in my hotel room one morning and was shaking. The reasons were clear enough. At the age of 37 I had debts of £2.8 million. I had a personal overdraft of £220,000. I had long-term interest debts and I had money tied up in Hearts. The whole picture gave me the fright of my life.

"For the next week in California I planned how to prevent the pack of cards falling down around me. And while all this was going on Hearts were under constant pressure," he said.

Mercer will not blame his business difficulties in the early 1980s on his involvement with Hearts, even though the Tynecastle operation took up so much of his time. In some respects he regarded the involvement in the football world as a therapeutic exercise. He found he was able to lose himself in the club's problems rather than dwelling so much on his own.

Having said that, with the benefit of hindsight Mercer knows that if he hadn't staked £275,000 to buy into the club and then made various loans to Hearts – in other words, if he'd kept his cash in his own business – he would never have got into such turmoil in the first place. "The money I put into Hearts almost broke me physically, mentally and financially," said Mercer. "But it was from the ashes of that situation that I was able to find myself. People wonder where the in-built strength of the club comes from. It is through the case-hardened experience of myself and Alex MacDonald and Sandy Jardine."

Mercer believes that having come through so much adversity there is more to Hearts than meets the eye. "When teams play Hearts, they don't realise that they are playing more than just the players on the field. There were times when we didn't have great players. But there was an inner strength, forged during those difficult times, which is still there today," he said.

Many of Mercer's business colleagues in 1982 regarded his involvement with a football club as a fundamental error of judgement. It is not hard to understand, six years on, given Hearts' place at the forefront of the Scottish game, why Mercer takes satisfaction in a gamble that paid off. "As far as Hearts are concerned, they've just announced profits for the sixth year running. As for Dunedin, they are the fastest-growing property company in Scotland, with assets in 1988 of £30 million and profits and reserves of £3 million," said Mercer.

CHAPTER SEVEN

Almost There

MIKE AITKEN

OFF THE FIELD, the good ideas kept on coming. The enlargement of the Junior Section and the allocation of part of the enclosure to encourage youngsters to watch football in a well-positioned, secure facility was another step forward for a club that was aware of the need to curtail the hooligan element that had threatened to destroy it a few years previously. Other schemes, such as the £5 discount card for supporters, didn't have any lasting impact, but at least enjoyed the virtue of maintaining the club's high profile.

There was some justification, though, for the school of thought that suggested it was about time Hearts did some serious talking on the field as well as in the boardroom. Winning a place in Europe at the first time of asking in the Premier Division in 1984 was as handsome a rejoinder as manager Alex MacDonald could have wished to fashion. For his efforts MacDonald was awarded a new contract and a testimonial match against Rangers. Some 18,000 spectators surged through the turnstiles at Tynecastle to see Kevin Keegan play for Hearts. They paid gate receipts of £36,000 in tribute to the player-manager. Sandy Jardine also signed a new contract at this point, so Hearts were well positioned to capitalise on a bright return to top ten football.

The re-emergence of the Edinburgh side in the Premier Division was not only good news for those with a vested interest in the affairs of the club, but also for the rest of the leading lights as Hearts pulled in 234,422 spectators and immediately became the fourth-best-supported team in the League after Rangers, Celtic and Aberdeen. In time only the "Old Firm" would have more customers. Operating in profit as a club, Hearts had new faces on the playing staff and a positive style of play that drew admiration from the local press. "A plum tie in Europe, an operating profit last season, a growing reputation as a soccer crowd-puller, and all of it achieved where it matters – by results on the field. Take a bow, Hearts," enthused one editorial.

Hearts' Junior Club has been a great success story – here the kids show (from left) John Colquhoun, Craig Levein, Sandy Jardine and Walter Kidd, how they feel about being at Tynecastle.

Unfortunately, the plum tie in question against Paris St Germain in the UEFA Cup represented rather too formidable a hurdle for a side not long out of the First Division. Nonetheless, the trip to Paris was a return to the big time for Hearts and a nostalgic trip for Mercer, who had played on the wing for London Scottish against Racing Club de Paris as a teenager. The rugby team, however, travelled in vain, and Hearts also found themselves on the wrong end of a 4-0 drubbing. More important, though, was the good behaviour of more than 3,000 Hearts fans, who made the trip to Paris and were praised by the mayor of that city for their conduct. Beforehand there had been dire warnings about a ban from Europe if the supporters stepped out of line.

A dozen so-called Hearts fans had run on to the pitch during the Edinburgh derby between Hibs and Hearts at Easter Road a couple of weeks prior to the European game. The behaviour of those who had invaded the pitch was condemned by Alex MacDonald as "scandalous." And Wallace Mercer called on fans to form their own police force on the terracings to weed out the troublemakers. Mercer was not impressed with the way the fixture was policed, but sensibly made no attempt to excuse the hooligans. At any rate, Hearts made the trip to France knowing that they could ill afford further incidents of misbehaviour. In fact both legs of the tie, which St Germain won handsomely, were superbly handled, and not a single supporter was arrested at either match. After the second leg at Tynecastle, Victor Lamaux, the UEFA observer from Belgium who had once come down like a ton of bricks on Brian Clough for calling the Polish goalkeeper Jan Tomaszewski "a clown," said that he was so impressed by the organisation at Tynecastle that he would submit his most complimentary report ever on a European match.

Mercer knew that Hearts had overstretched themselves against Paris St Germain and immediately set about trying to answer a number of questions. How quickly could the club bridge the gap between those players around the age of 20 and those over 30? Could Hearts hang on to all their talented youngsters? And what could be done to prevent sectarianism and hooliganism taking root amongst the club's growing support?

As evidence of their commitment to retaining their best players, Hearts turned down a £400,000 offer from Spurs for John Robertson. The management team also appreciated that the "Dad's Army" brigade – Willie Johnston was 37, Jimmy Bone 35 – would soon have to call it a day. As for the question of hooliganism, Mercer believed it was a social problem rather than a football problem, but was enough of a pragmatist to understand that it was also a Hearts problem. He planned to take various steps to eliminate the disreputable element that had attached itself to the club. However, the SFA's plan to deduct points from Hearts as a punishment for spectators coming on to the pitch at Easter Road drew Mercer's wrath. He eventually won his point, and Hearts were not even fined for the events at Easter Road. Instead, the SFA and the Scottish League decided to set up a joint disciplinary commission on hooliganism. The Hearts chairman welcomed the development but pointed out that "we and other clubs have a major social problem on our hands. We are living in a time of great unrest which manifests itself in our football grounds. The setting up of the commission was a step forward, but we needed more help from the judiciary to control it."

The next time Hearts played Hibs, Mercer publicly stated the club's opposition to sectarianism. "We want to make our ground a place of family entertainment, but cannot do that if parents are frightened for the safety of their children," he said. Video cameras, plain clothes police, extra stewards and strengthened perimeter fencing were all introduced in a bid to back sentiment with action. The cameras worked so well that Hearts went on to become the first club in Scotland to introduce closed circuit television on a permanent basis. The Football Trust footed the bill for £35,000 and director Pilmar Smith stressed: "No one has the complete answer to fighting the hooligan element, but we are trying to do our utmost." Hearts, in short, were winning the war against hooliganism, and Wallace Mercer took part in an ITV documentary on the recommendation of Scottish Office ministers as an example of what could be achieved by those who had a mind to. As Chelsea and Milwall fans went on the rampage south of the border,

Dave Bowman (left) did the club a favour by moving when he did as the cash from his transfer was much needed at the time.

Mercer told the *Sunday Times*: "I wouldn't want to run a club that was a blight on the community and I don't want to see governments running football. Once the FA takes the bull by the horns and creates a collective willingness among the English fans to behave, they will find that mood carries itself forward." Mercer's advocacy of the strides taken by Hearts in particular and Scottish football in general also found a national airing on the Jimmy Young show on Radio Two.

Hearts, meantime, were striving to cope with their financial difficulties. The sale of David Bowman to Coventry for £200,000 enabled the club to give their players a wage rise as well as funding the purchase of Andy Watson from Leeds United. "Frankly, David Bowman did the club a greater service by leaving than others in the past have done by staying," said Mercer. "Having been in the first team for four years, he'd made his contribution. His departure gave us more financial options – and that satisfied us because the club isn't run for the benefit of the management or the directors. It is run for the players and the fans, and every penny we raised we ploughed back into the team."

Winning the Tennent's Sixes, an indoor tournament staged at Ingliston at the start of 1985, was small beer by most standards, but a 4-1 win over Morton in the final was important for reasons other than a trophy and a cheque for £7,000. It was the first success of any sort since the new régime had taken over almost four years previously, and gave the club's supporters something to shout about. Here at last was a visible sign of better days to come.

Mercer's involvement as a council member of the SFA and a member of the Scottish League's management committee was rarely without outbursts of controversy. The Hearts chairman has always been a man to speak his mind, and such straight shooting did not endear him to the hierarchy. For instance, when the Scottish League announced a sponsorship deal with Fine Fare worth £250,000, Mercer was up in arms about the decision to give the Premier Division clubs just £10,000 each. He argued that 80 per cent of the cash should go to the top ten.

Given the success Mercer had enjoyed as an eloquent spokesman for Hearts, it was not surprising that there was speculation around the spring of 1985 that the Tynecastle chairman might be lured to take over at Ibrox. Before David Holmes restored Rangers' pre-eminent place in the Scottish game, the club was directionless. Some thought that the appointment of Mercer as chief executive would add purpose. While Mercer said he would have to think about such a move if it ever came about, no formal approach was ever made and John Paton, then the chairman of Rangers, denied the rumours. In fact the prospect of

Captain Walter Kidd holds aloft the Tennent's sixes trophy at Ingliston in 1985.

Mercer considering leaving Hearts caused considerable alarm amongst the club's supporters, and season ticket sales nose-dived. Eventually the chairman publicly declared that some people had taken the story more seriously than he did and, whatever had been said to the contrary, he was with Hearts to stay.

There was more controversy involving Hearts and Rangers when the teams met in a game dubbed "The Battle of Ibrox." Three players, Walter Kidd and Sandy Clark of Hearts and Ally McCoist of Rangers, were sent off after a brawl, and eight other players were booked. Perhaps anticipating the involvement of the procurator-fiscal in years to come, Mercer said: "Had people on the terracing behaved in the same way they could have ended up in jail or at the very least been heavily fined. I was embarrassed by what happened, and so were Hearts football club. It won't happen again." Nonetheless, when Kidd and Clark appealed against an additional punishment – SFA secretary Ernie Walker branded them as hooligans – by taking the matter to court, it was an unprecedented move to get a decision of the SFA's disciplinary committee overturned by the Court of Session. In fact Lord Mayfield dismissed the players' case against a three-match suspension, refusing to grant interim interdict on the grounds that any intervention from the courts could jeopardise the authority of the SFA. He added that this would have had adverse and serious consequences for the future of the game.

Whatever was happening at Tynecastle, the big story during the 1985/86 season was the long-running breakaway saga. Perhaps the controversy started when I wrote an exclusive article for the *Scotsman* outlining the Aberdeen vice-chairman Chris Anderson's views on setting up a Scottish National League that would harness the game's financial resources – the money from television, sponsorship and the Football Trust – in order to help to raise standards and ensure a meaningful future for the full-time game in Scotland. "My feeling is that with ten clubs we hardly have a league at all," said Anderson. "Not that I'm arguing for a return to the old ways or a championship like Portugal's which regularly produce Europe's top goalscorer because the overall quality of opposition is modest. We don't want to go down that road again. What we do want is a quality league. Because if we are serious about our football, even with our small resources in Scotland, and want to compete with the best in Europe, then this is the direction we need to move in to progress."

The gulf between the Premier Division's leading lights and the Scottish League shortly came to a head, ostensibly over a row about live television coverage of a game between Rangers and Celtic. In fact the divisions between both sides were much greater than first met the uneducated eye. What was being debated was the very future of Scottish football.

Mercer, who represented the Premier Division clubs on the League management committee, was bitterly opposed to moves that would have allowed the Scottish League to decide who had the right to enter grounds. "If the proposals I have seen in draft are passed," Mercer said, "they will remove the right of individual clubs to decide who or what enters their ground. In effect, we would no longer be able to manage our own affairs. We might have to consider a breakaway league even if it means losing a place in UEFA."

Wallace Mercer with David Will, President of the Scottish Football Association.

Hearts never had any intention of pulling out of the Scottish League on their own – a suggestion Mercer dismissed as "crass stupidity" – but after a meeting at Tynecastle involving Rangers, Celtic, Aberdeen, Hearts, Hibs and Motherwell, where the clubs were joined by the Dean of the Faculty of Advocates, William Prossor, Mercer stressed that the position was very serious. Campbell Ogilvy, the secretary of Rangers, said in a statement; "The six clubs considered that major changes in the structure of the league are required regardless of the current television problems. These changes could be achieved either within the existing league or outwith it."

Of course, the dissident six were always more interested in reorganising Scottish football than abandoning it. But as both sides became more and more entrenched, it looked for a while as if a breakaway might be a genuine possibility. Dundee, Dundee United and St Mirren eventually joined the six, and at a meeting in Perth went so far as to draw up a constitution and inform the Scottish League of their decision to quit that organisation in May of 1986. The key to the problem was that the composition of the Premier Division with a fifth of its membership relegated never gave ambitious clubs either the stability or the incentive to invest in the future. The parochialism of those in the lower reaches of the League meant that the minnows failed to comprehend the extent to which they were jeopardising the game's future in Scotland by their backwater attitude to change.

In spite of peace moves initiated by Ian Gellatly, the president of the Scottish League, and warning shots from the SFA about the consequences of breaking away, a fresh start for Scottish football seemed inevitable until an unseemly compromise was eventually hammered out. While the big guns got most of what they were asking for in terms of financial clout, the reorganisation of the Premier Division into a 12-club league for two seasons was a serious mistake. It inflicted far too many games on players and spectators alike. If the goal was a ten-club league with only one team relegated and one promoted, a better system than this administrative nightmare could surely have been concocted.

When peace eventually broke out between the Scottish League and the rebel nine, Hearts were in the remarkable position of leading the Premier Division championship and looking forward to a Scottish Cup final appearance against Aberdeen at Hampden. These stirring times were chronicled in a book I edited entitled *Glorious Hearts*, while John Fairgrieve penned *The Boys in Maroon*. Both publications told the story of a side that almost won the double of League and Cup and ended up with nothing apart from pride in performance to show for their efforts. While Aberdeen won the Scottish Cup, Celtic pipped Hearts for the title. But whatever was lost in terms of silverware – the defeat at Dens Park after a run of 31 unbeaten games was one of the most emotional moments in the club's history – Hearts had gained the respect of the community.

In a leading article the *Scotsman* declared: "It was only right and proper that a Hearts player should be named as Footballer of the Year. When Sandy Jardine received the Scottish Football Writers' annual award, he was receiving it not only as a recognition of his own outstanding contribution on the field, but as a tribute to the collective

A typical Hearts celebration in season 1986-87.

effort of the Hearts side over a quite remarkable season. On Saturday
the cussed fighting men of Dundee ended the Edinburgh team's
astonishing unbeaten run and in so doing deprived Hearts of the

Premier Division title which had seemed theirs for the taking. The spell which had held a city – or a good part of it – in thrall for months was broken, the warm dream cruelly blown away by the bitter disappointment of stunning defeat. Amid the disappointment, however, the real gains of Hearts' season should not be forgotten. Under the ebullient chairmanship of Wallace Mercer and the young management team of Alex MacDonald and Jardine the club has been restored to vigorous health. Where, not so long ago, all was stagnation and lethargy, there is now excitement and life."

Whatever the disappointments Hearts felt at the time – and a reaction did set in during the 1986/87 season – Mercer maintains that the work that has been done at Tynecastle goes beyond the winning of trophies. "It is irrelevant to me whether we win a cup or secure the League flag," he said. "Of course you want to see that happen for the players and the supporters, and our aim here is to do everything to give them that, but we've won many cups and flags here – for our success has been in pulling a club out of the gutter. We went from being ranked 15th in Scottish football when we were relegated to being among the first two or three.

"Before taking over as chairman of Hearts I was the youngest chairman of Edinburgh Pentlands Round Table. I mention that, because in my own way I'd always had a social conscience. I've never wavered in those attitudes, and since I walked in the door at Tynecastle the one thing I wouldn't tolerate was indiscipline – either on the field from my players or off the field from the supporters.

"When I came to Tynecastle the club had a major social problem, which was partly linked to the lack of performance on the field and partly to bigotry. The first day I joined the club I was invited to join the Masons. My father was a Mason and I wouldn't say anything to criticise that organisation. But I decided the moment I took over the mantle of responsibility for Hearts that it would be a non-religious, non-political club. Since then I've followed that course, irrespective of my own private views.

"I am absolutely ruthless when it comes to these issues cf religion and behaviour. I expect certain standards, and from the beginning I knew that the club didn't need what was happening off the field. From day one we've set out our stall, and there's no doubt that Pilmar Smith has played a major role. It is a cause we worked on for six years or so.

"You don't want to sound as if you're beating your own drum, but in dealing with the problem of hooliganism, as in a number of other areas, this club was a trail-blazer. We were the first to appoint a player-manager, the first to appoint a director to represent the fans, the first to bus our support to away games and the first to let the unemployed in for nothing. We've always been innovative because there was so much that had to be looked into at the club. Now others have taken up a lot of our ideas. I suppose we should be pleased. After all, they say imitation is the sincerest form of flattery."

Hearts' supporters have greatly improved their image over the years – here a section of fans took to fancy dress for a visit to Ibrox.

CHAPTER EIGHT

The Players

MIKE AITKEN

THE MODERN FOOTBALLER lives in his own home, believes in equality of the sexes, enjoys going out for a meal, doesn't smoke, plays golf for relaxation and thinks about investing his hard-earned cash in stocks and shares. Outwith football he's most interested in setting up his own business.

It may not quite reflect the typical yuppie profile – our average player will vote Labour rather than Conservative – but the findings of a poll of full-time professionals employed by Hearts indicates a comprehensive endorsement of goals and values usually categorised as middle-class. Like folk in most walks of life, footballers believe they work hard and provide good value for money for the salaries they earn. Players say they help around the house and that if their football career came to an end, most would attempt to go into business for themselves.

More than half of the players who took part in the survey were interested in politics and current events, 25% listed reading as a hobby and 95% read at least one newspaper every day. Fifty percent of the players said they planned to vote Labour at the next general election, while 20% were Tories. There was less interest in local politics, however, with 55% not likely to vote in local elections. As far as their livelihood was concerned, the main attraction for the players of participating in the Premier Division was the size of the crowds. Whatever the recent success story of Scottish football, some 80% of the survey said that at some point they'd like to pursue their career either in England or abroad.

As was to be expected from a group of professionals, winning and losing were the biggest likes and dislikes in the game, though a surprisingly high percentage rated playing well as the greater source of satisfaction. None of those polled rated entertaining the fans as the main priority, which must tell us something about the competitive nature of modern sport.

For me football is about players and supporters – but the most important people of all are the playing staff. Here is Hearts' line-up, season 1987-88.

The physical nature of the top ten and the growing emphasis on robust play encouraged 50% of the players to express the view that creative players don't receive adequate protection in matches. It seems, however, that familiarity rather than fear is perceived as the main deficiency of the top ten. No fewer than 75% of the players complained that they meet the same teams too often.

Referees are held in low esteem by the players, with 85% voicing the opinion that officials are inconsistent while another 15% think that standards have dropped in recent years. Players are also unimpressed by the way football is run by the authorities, with 70% saying that the SFA and the Scottish League could do a better job. The Players Union doesn't escape censure either, as 65% of the players stated the view that more could be done by that organisation to help the players, while 10% even thought the association was irrelevant. (The poll took place before the Union announced plans to set up an educational trust and improve insurance benefits for members.)

Some 90% of the players would like to stay on in football in some capacity, either as a manager or a coach, after their playing careers are over. They regarded themselves as earning a fair wage, although 15% felt that managers were overpaid.

Interestingly, the prospect of a British League, which has been in the air again, appealed to 75% of the players. Skill was regarded as the most important asset a top-quality player could possess, with mental and physical toughness rated above speed.

Most players supported the status quo as far as the televising of matches was concerned. No one thought that there was too much football on television and 35% felt that more live games should be shown in Scotland. Some 35% of the players listed watching television as one of their hobbies or interests outwith the game, though far and away the most popular pastime was golf – 80% of the playing staff take to the fairways of their local club in search of relaxation.

The tendency to view footballers as male chauvinists is exposed as a myth: 90% of the players said they helped around the house and 80% said that in marriage men and women should be equal partners. For 85% of the players the ideal night out was going to a restaurant for a meal. Only 10% preferred a party.

Every individual who took part in the survey either had a mortgage or wanted to own his own home. Mrs Thatcher's ambition to make us a nation of shareholders was reflected in the fact that 30% of the players had either bought shares or invested money in the stock market.

There wasn't one member of the squad who smoked, and only 5% of the staff held the view that the modern footballer drank more than his predecessors.

John Colquhoun, who has made no secret of his interest in politics and plays an active role in the affairs of the Players Union, expanded on the limited choice answers by making a number of additional observations of his own.

He didn't think that the reporting of football could be pigeon-holed as either sensational or accurate since "newspapers are all directed at different readerships". Freedom of contract, which 80% of the players supported, was welcomed by Colquhoun as "good, especially for the cream of the game, although I don't think it has been harmful to any player". The possibility of a British League was assessed by the 24-year-old forward as potentially "good for the top clubs but a disaster for the smaller ones". Not surprisingly, given the Players Union's wish to see 10% of all money from television go to help safeguard the welfare of the Association's membership, John Colquhoun thought that "a lot more could be done with the finance from the TV monies". Colquhoun observed that it would surely be for the betterment of the game's organisation if it was administered by one body, not two – SFA and the League – as is the case at present. And as far as the consumption of alcohol was concerned, Colquhoun stressed: "I don't think footballers drink more or less than any other body of men."

Here are the findings of the poll in full:
Survey
1. What do you enjoy most about playing football?
A Winning 70%   *B* Playing well 30%   *C* Entertaining the fans 0%.

I regarded John Colquhoun as our most valuable player in 1987-88. Here the internationalist takes on the St Mirren defence.

2. What do you dislike most about playing football?
A Foul play 5%   B Making mistakes 10%   C Losing 85%.

3. Do you think creative players get adequate protection in the modern game?
A Yes 35%   B No 50%   C Don't know 15%.

4. What's the main drawback about playing in the Premier Division?
A Too many games 15%   B Physical play 5%   C Meeting the same team too often 75% D None of these 5%.

5. What's the great attraction of playing in the Premier Division?
A Increased competition 25%   B Quality football 25%   C Larger crowds 50%.

6. What do you think of present refereeing standards?
A Inconsistent 85%   B The best in Europe 0%   C Not as good as before 15%.

7. Given the chance of a move, ideally would you prefer –
A To stay in Scotland 20%   B Play in England 40%   C Play abroad 40%.

8. What do you think of the way football is reported by newspapers?
A Accurately 20%   B Sensationally 55%   C Don't read them 10% D None of these 15%.

9. What's your opinion of television coverage of football?
A There should be more live games 35%   B Existing coverage is about right 65%   C There's too much football on TV 0%.

10. What would you do if your career in football ended?
A Set up your own business 60%   B Learn another trade 15%   C Not thought about it 25%.

11. If you had the chance to stay on in football, would you like to become a manager or coach?
A Yes 90%   B No 5%   C Don't know 5%.

12. What's your opinion of freedom of contract?
A A good thing 80%   B A bad idea 5%   C Don't know 15%.

13. What do you think of the prospect of a British League?
A A good idea 75%   B A bad move 10%   C Don't know 15%.

14. What quality matters most to a modern footballer?
A Skill 50%   B Mental and physical toughness 30%   C Speed 20%.

15. What's your opinion of the way football authorities run the game in Scotland?
A They do a good job 15%   B Could do much better 70%   C Don't know 15%.

16. What do you think of the Players Union?

A Does a good job 25%   *B* Could do more 65%   *C* Not relevant 10%.

17. What's your opinion of a footballer's earnings?
A Overpaid 0%   *B* Earn a fair wage 85%   *C* Underpaid 15%.

18. What do you think of a manager's rewards?
A Overpaid 15%   *B* Earn a fair wage 70%   *C* Underpaid 5%
D Don't know 10%.

19. What do you think of the demands made of a footballer?
A Work hard 95%   *B* Don't work hard enough 5%.

20. How do you intend to vote at the next general election?
A SNP 5%   *B* Labour 50%   *C* Conservative 20%   *D* Alliance 0%
E Don't know 25%.

21. Do you vote in local elections?
A Yes 45%   *B* No 55%.

22. Do you take an interest in politics and current events?
A Yes 55%   *B* No 45%.

23. Do you read newspapers?
A Yes 95%   *B* No 5%.

24. What hobbies or interests do you have outside football?
A Golf 80%   *B* Squash 25%   *C* Reading 25%   *D* Watching
television 35%   *E* Horse Racing 35%   *F* DIY 25%   *G* Music 25%
H Cars 15%   *I* Swimming 15%.

25. At home, do you help around the house?
A Yes 90%   *B* No 10%.

26. For entertainment, what do you prefer to do?
A Go out for a meal 85%   *B* Go to a party 10%   *C* Go to the cinema
or theatre 5%   *D* Stay at home 0%.

27. Who should be the boss in a marriage?
A The man 20%   *B* The woman 0%   *C* Equal partners 80%.

28. Do you have a mortgage or would like to own your own home?
A Yes 100%   *B* No 0%.

29. Have you ever bought shares or invested money in the stock market?
A Yes 30%   *B* No 70%.

30. What do you think of modern footballers' drinking habits?
A Drink less than before 20%   *B* More than in the past 5%   *C* Don't
know 75%.

31. What do you think of the timing of the football season?
A Should be a winter break 15%   *B* Fine as it is 65%   *C* Should play
in the summer 20%.

32. Do you smoke?
A Yes 0%   *B* No 100%.

The full time professional players who took part in the survey were:-
Gary Mackay (24), signed in 1980, from Salvesen B.C.; Mark Gavin
(24), signed in 1988, from Rochdale; Mike Galloway (22), signed in
1987, from Halifax; Malcolm Murray (23), signed in 1983, from Buckie
Thistle; Alan Moore (23), signed in 1986, from Dumbarton; Sandy
Jardine (39), signed in 1982, from Rangers; Ian Jardine (30), signed in
1985, from Anorthosis, Cyprus; Walter Kidd (30), signed in 1978,
from Newtongrange Star; Scott Crabbe (19), signed in 1986, from
Tynecastle B.C.; Sandy Clark (31), signed in 1984, from Rangers;
John Robertson (23), signed in 1981, from from Edina Hibs (left for
Newcastle United in April 1988); Andy Bruce (23), signed in 1987,
from Rangers; Brian Whittaker (31), signed in 1984, from Celtic; Dave
McPherson (24), signed in 1987, from Rangers; Henry Smith (32),
signed in 1981, from Leeds Utd; Craig Levein (23), signed in 1983,
from Cowdenbeath; Wayne Foster (24), signed in 1986, from Bolton
Wanderers; Neil Berry (25), signed in 1984, from Bolton Wanderers;
John Colquhoun (24), signed in 1985, from Celtic.

CHAPTER NINE

Good Habits

MIKE AITKEN

A NEW PLAYER arriving at Tynecastle in the summer might be taken aback to find that the ground is almost as active during the close season as it is from August to May. The management team of Alex MacDonald and Sandy Jardine don't believe in the lazy, hazy, crazy days of summer for their players and, like good athletes, expect them to keep in trim.

According to Sandy Jardine, the value of the close season lies in helping jaded players to find a freshness of mind. Once the last ball of the old season has been kicked, Hearts foresee their players enjoying a fortnight of complete rest. After they've been able to put their feet up for a spell, players find that the aches and pains have disappeared and it is time to keep their fitness level ticking over.

As the door of Tynecastle is always open, players are encouraged to come in twice a week. Jardine and MacDonald believe it is vital that their players accept self-responsibility and, as a consequence, don't impose rigid schedules. However, the individual who made no attempt to keep himself fit during the summer would be bound to suffer badly when it came time to take part in the pre-season training schedule.

Since there are no matches to be played during the summer, players don't require an edge to their fitness, and it can be an important time for those in need of building up their strength and stamina. Equally, MacDonald and Jardine are unconcerned if individuals want to go out and enjoy themselves during the close season. Behaviour that would be

97

regarded as unacceptable once the season starts is regarded as an
important part of the winding-down process during the summer.

The late nights and the socialising, however, become a thing of the
past when the pre-season work gets under way. "When we bring the
players in to start work in earnest for the new season we don't believe in
easing them back. In my early days as a player at Ibrox, you'd start off
with the odd game of crab football and baseball. Times have changed,
and when our players come in on that first morning they know for sure it
is going to be hard graft," said Jardine. Given that Alex MacDonald at
40 was the second-oldest registered player on the books of a Premier
Division club in 1988 – another Ibrox old boy, Willie Johnston, was still
playing for Falkirk reserves at 41 – and that Sandy Jardine was named as
Scotland's player of the year by the Scottish Football Writers'
Association for the second time at 37, the Hearts management team set
a good example to their players of the value of maintaining a high level
of fitness.

*Back to work – after the summer break the players and manager get down to a
sprint session at Moray House playing fields.*

"There is no reason why players shouldn't keep fit all the year round," Alex MacDonald added. "After all, the body is a muscle. The more you work at it the stronger it will get. The basic thing about the close season is to keep ticking over. And the players get a sense of satisfaction from keeping themselves right. In addition, if you go into a demanding period of pre-season training after seven or eight weeks of doing nothing, then you are bound to pick up a lot of strains. It will also be an agonising experience for the person who hasn't kept himself right.

"Our players appreciate the value of achieving a high level of fitness. Our programme is designed to help players reap the maximum benefit from the effort they put in. That's why such a good spirit surrounds the work we do in training. The players understand that what we're asking them to do isn't a burden for them but something which can give them a sense of accomplishment. All our lads are good trainers, which is just as well, because Tynecastle is the worst place to earn your living if you are a bad one."

The pre-season schedule consists of ten days' hard running designed to build stamina and strength which will be on tap throughout the campaign that lies ahead. Only after that do MacDonald and Jardine begin to sharpen their players and start to look for an edge. The emphasis in this phase switches to the recovery and the honing of a player's touch.

Hearts like to get at least six matches under their belt before the new season proper starts in August. In their early days at Tynecastle, MacDonald and Jardine didn't have the funds to take the players abroad, and instead Hearts would get away from their normal environment to the North of Scotland, where facilities were good and hospitality was warm. The success of recent years, however, has meant that MacDonald and Jardine can offer their first-team squad the same kind of opportunities they enjoyed as players themselves with Rangers. "Alex and I thoroughly enjoyed going abroad to train with Rangers. But these tours are expensive operations to mount, and it is only in the last four years that we've been able to go to places like West Germany. The good thing about travelling to that part of Europe is that even if you are playing amateur teams, they've got excellent facilities and perform to a remarkably high standard. The playing surfaces couldn't be better and, thanks to the winter shut-down, all their players are match-fit. Consequently you are not only getting a change of environment, but also truly hard games, whatever the opposition," said Jardine.

Hearts enjoy the opportunity in West Germany, away from the attention that would surround them at home, to experiment with different formations and new players. The club have tried to add a couple of players to the staff during each close season in recent years and a trip abroad for ten days or so offers the ideal means of educating an incomer in the ways of his new employers. It is also an opportunity for MacDonald and Jardine to discover things about the individual that would not be obvious to an outsider.

Once the season proper slips into action, Hearts believe firmly in the value of routine and expect their players to adhere to a disciplined schedule throughout the footballing year. "On a Monday morning we're looking for the players to get the aches and the bruises out of their system," said Jardine. "How we judge the thing depends on the mood – are the players down because we've been beaten, or up after we've played well and won? We also start to have chats with players who might have done something wrong or could improve on some aspect of their game that had let them down.

"We don't believe in having a general discussion about the match we've just played. If we're going to point things out to people it has to be done in the right way. The only occasion when we might feel the need of a get-together of that nature would be when the club had suffered a sequence of bad results. It is not something we make a habit of. Frankly, when your side is going reasonably well, you don't need it.

"We prefer to point things out to individuals, and there is also an opportunity at team talks to make general observations. After matches we always sit the players down and usually have things to tell them. Sometimes you'll give them stick, or on the other hand you'll give them a bit of praise. It is an important time to make an observation to a player because the game is still fresh in his mind. By Monday it is time to take a player aside and explain to him more fully what he's done wrong and how to rectify it. Other than that, the start of the week isn't a time for heavy training or post-mortems."

As a rule, Hearts put their players through the stiffest session of the week on a Tuesday, though such a demanding work-out is hardly appropriate when the club have a Wednesday fixture to fulfil. If there isn't any midweek football, then the Hearts players can expect a tough, physical programme with no ball work. The first-team squad begin with running exercises and move on to speedball circuit in the gym. When there's no Wednesday night match, Hearts will often give their players a day off in the middle of the week in order to allow them to recover from their exertions on Tuesday.

By Thursday the training schedule is starting to focus on Saturday's match. Players work in boxes and there is an emphasis on the one- and two-touch football that epitomises Hearts' style of support play. Practice matches are also staged for 15 minutes or so in order to illustrate how the opposition may approach the game and the best way to go about handling it.

Neil Berry is a powerhouse in Hearts' midfield as he shrugs off a challenge from Iain Durrant of Rangers.

On Friday the Hearts players do short sprints, and the management team aim to create a light-hearted mood at the session. And on match day, there's a 45-minute loosening-up session before the coaching staff work with the players on corners, free kicks and throw-ins. During the warm-up MacDonald and Jardine tell the players the team for that afternoon's match. If a player has been left out for some reason or other, Hearts don't leave him in the dark as to why he's been omitted. "We prefer to take an individual aside and let him know privately rather than speak in front of all the players," said MacDonald.

Hearts believe that their players should consider themselves as athletes as much as footballers, and consequently there is a special emphasis on routine and following a systematic training programme. "All the best professional athletes know what they're doing in that respect, and it is important for our players in helping them to plan their week. Routine is vital for a sportsman. In saying that, while our players will know they're going to get a hard day on a Tuesday, they won't know specifically what they're going to get. That's an important part of our job in the course of a long season. We've got to come up with ideas that keep the players fresh. It is not just about training people hard. To do that isn't difficult. The knack is knowing when to rest players as well as to work them. Sometimes you might even surprise them by saying 'Have a couple of days off'. Always, though, you want to keep players on their toes. Yes, it is necessary for players to have a routine, but within that routine there must be an element of uncertainty about what's coming next. Otherwise players can become stale," said Jardine.

Hearts have a magpie attitude towards training methods, and will always watch carefully how others go about things in case there is something new to be learned. "The bottom line is that there are only so many ways in which you can shoot to score a goal, only so many ways you can head the ball, and only so many ways you can pass it. Whatever you're trying to achieve, the game boils down to someone trying to get the ball into the net. In that respect it is a very simple game, but also one that can have a complicated dimension," added the manager.

While MacDonald and Jardine attract the attention of the public and the media, both men are quick to pay tribute to the coaching skills of Walter Borthwick. A former player with St Mirren and Dunfermline, where he also did some coaching, Borthwick had made a career for himself in the civil service before Hearts offered him the chance of taking the job of first-team coach. Borthwick took the gamble of a full-time involvement in the game, and is now regarded behind the scenes as a significant figure in Hearts' revival. "Walter is involved in a lot of the coaching courses and sees many things that can help us," Jardine went on. "He's exceptionally good at setting things up in training. Whether we want to set up shooting or crossing exercises or whatever, Wattie will have an idea to do it in a different way. It is true Alex and I get all the publicity, but no one should underestimate Wattie's role at Tynecastle."

Away from the training ground Hearts may not stage blackboard lectures, but MacDonald and Jardine are both firm believers in the value of talking to players. Individuals will be taken aside, possibly while working on something else, and given information about the player they can expect to come up against on the Saturday.

Wayne Foster (right) is another bargain signing whose pace and courage have been assets to the club.

On a more general basis, at the team talk before a match, Hearts' management team will linger on the techniques of the opposition. Jardine and MacDonald dwell on the pattern their opponents play to, and there is a thorough examination of strengths and weaknesses. "We always try to think about what the opposition are going to do, but we always cover ourselves with the players by reminding them that the other team might change things. The important thing here is to be flexible. We want to give our players a fair idea of what to expect. But should something different crop up, then it is vital that they are not fazed by that. Most of the time you tend to get things right in advance, but there's no way you want to stereotype your players. Within a framework of a team game, they've got to keep their minds open and be able to think for themselves," said Jardine.

Like most managers, MacDonald and Jardine hold to the philosophy that the key to any game is how their own side plays. "What we stress to our players is that if everyone in the team plays well, then in our opinion there are not many teams around that can beat us. The focus of all our work during the week is designed to get our team to give its best on the day. If we can do that, then it doesn't matter all that much what the opposition do. You want your players to have all the required information about the opposition, but at the end of the day it is how we play that matters," he added.

Nonetheless Hearts, on occasion, do change their team around to minimise the effectiveness of a potentially dangerous opponent. "If someone is going to give one of our players a problem, then you use that to play to your strengths by taking that problem away. We'll never ignore a problem in advance, and we are quite prepared to make a change if it will help the team," said Jardine.

During the half-time interval of a match, the Hearts players return to the dressing-room, take a seat and get a cup of tea. MacDonald and Jardine go through the players both as a team and as individuals. When things haven't gone well, the players can expect a rocket. On the other hand, there could be praise for a good performance. But even when the side is winning, Hearts' management team take the view that there are things that could be done even better.

Some individuals will get a gee-up, and under certain circumstances it may be necessary to fire and motivate the entire team. There will be discussion of how to rectify a problem that the opposition may be causing the team. "What's said at half-time is very important," said Jardine. "And what we're trying to achieve is to ensure that individuals do better in the second half. How you go about that depends on the nature of the player. There are various ways of effecting that change for the better. Some players you might put your arm around, others you might have to go through them. You can use fancy names like psychology if you like, but what we're really talking about is common sense. There's no use shouting and bawling at someone if it is going to have the opposite effect to the one you intended. Because the bottom line for a manager is that you do whatever you need to do in order to get more out of the team."

In the dressing-room at half-time and full-time the criticism that is handed out to certain players would shock most outsiders. Some very pointed remarks are made, and the language can be colourful. Alex MacDonald explained that in order to help the players to deal with criticism he would tell them the basis on which it was handed out. "We say to them that nothing is personal. You can't take things the wrong way. You've got to have a thick skin. From our point of view, if you leave someone without a name and it helps the team to win, then the end justifies the means."

New players at Tynecastle are always taken aside and told how the management team operate. If there is criticism, it is not meant on a personal basis. The purpose is to help the team to achieve better results.

"We're not trying to score points off people," MacDonald added. "Everything we do is geared to getting the best out of the team. Sometimes you give it your best shot, you do pretty well and you still get beaten. We can accept that. At the end of the day no one has a divine right to win all the time. When players give their best and you get beaten by a better side, then you hold your hand up and say 'Well done'. All we can do is try harder next time."

The influence exerted by the management team on the players once a match is under way is similar to that of the director of a play at a dress rehearsal. MacDonald and Jardine can't stop the action, but they do pass on information to their players. If the performance doesn't measure up – or the information isn't acted upon – then, star turn or not, an individual can find himself substituted. "In many ways, making a change in personnel is the last throw of the dice," said Jardine. "Obviously you start with the team that you think is best for the job. When things are not going well you've got the opportunity at half-time to try and sort matters out. And if that doesn't work then you think about putting on a substitute."

Whatever the outcome of a match, MacDonald and Jardine always make a point of sitting their players down in the dressing-room afterwards. By its nature, football produces a stream of highs and lows. There will be times after a game when the mood is one of elation. On a different day it could be disappointment or frustration that prevails. "No matter how well you've played, there's always something to learn," Jardine went on. "The observations we make to the players, whether it's praise or criticism, are to one end. They should help to make us a better team in future. Immediately after a game, however, isn't the time to explain things to players in depth. You can do that on Monday morning. Emotions run high after matches, and what you say at the time needs to be reinforced the following week.

"But the thing about working with good players is that you don't need to tell them five or six times. You tell them once or twice and they act upon it. The difficult part of a manager's job is dealing with individuals who don't seem to take things in. And you have to keep repeating and repeating and try and hammer the point home. You can't give up because there's always the chance that one time the message will get through and stick," said Jardine.

Outwith the activities of the first-team squad, MacDonald and Jardine have to monitor the progress of young men in the reserves, and there are numerous times when the two pools train together. There are days when the first team work on their own – mainly because their skill level is higher – but Hearts' management team are firm believers in the value of educating youngsters through their association with older professionals. "Young players don't just learn from good coaches, they learn from good pros," said MacDonald. "If young lads see that the first team have good habits, then they'll know that's the right way of doing things."

Sandy Jardine recalled that in his early days at Ibrox, nothing advanced his career more than the opportunity to work with players of the calibre of Jim Baxter and company. "It is important to give the youngsters that opportunity, though you must never lose sight of the fact that the club is determined by what the first team achieves on a Saturday. And there will always be times when you need to take the first team away on their own," he said.

Jardine and MacDonald both adhere to the view that there is an onus on them to put out the best team available to the club each week. "If you don't do that in the Premier Division, then you're kidding yourself," said Jardine. "It is such a competitive set-up that a club near the bottom can beat one near the top if you don't get it right. That's why age doesn't come into it. Whether they're young or old you put out the blend that makes your best team. We don't go with the thinking that you can't put a player in if he's too young. All that matters is quality.

"That's one of the reasons we've been able to attract a high calibre of youngster to Tynecastle. They know that if they're good enough then they'll get a chance with us. In addition, we try to foster a family atmosphere, and good habits are passed on from one generation of players to the next. The lads in their early 20s might not appreciate it at the moment, but by the time they get to their 30s they'll thank us for the work we've done with them."

Before injury intervened, Craig Levein was the jewel in Hearts' crown and a £750,000 bid for his services was turned down.

CHAPTER TEN

For the Game's Sake

MIKE AITKEN

W HEN GARY MACKAY made his international debut for Scotland
against Bulgaria in Sofia in 1987 and became the first Hearts
player to score for his country since Alex Young, the goal not
only made the 24-year-old midfield player a celebrity in Dublin
(Scotland's 1-0 win helped to send Eire to the European Championship
finals), it also marked the beginning of a new period of maturity in his
play that was to lead to his appointment as team captain.

It was a remarkable turnaround of events for Mackay, whose
confidence and form had dipped to such a low ebb in season 1986/87
that Hearts contemplated selling the player to Newcastle United.
Instead, both sides worked out their differences and Mackay signed a
new contract that will keep him at Tynecastle until 1990 – ten years on
from the day Archie Martin and Bobby Moncur secured his signature as
a 16-year-old in the summer of 1980.

If it had not been for his mother's illness, Gary Mackay would almost
certainly have signed for Manchester United that year. A former pupil
of Tynecastle Secondary who had played juvenile football with Salvesens, Mackay was one of the most sought after schoolboys in the
country. He reached a gentlemen's agreement to join the Old Trafford
club, and when news of his mother's illness reached Manchester United
they were so keen to sign him that they offered to let him stay at home,
train with the Scottish club of his choice and travel south to play each
Friday. It was a generous and thoughtful proposal from one of Britain's

most prestigious clubs. On the face of things, signing for Hearts at a time when even the teenage Mackay appreciated that the Edinburgh club was in a shambolic state didn't make a lot of sense. But when Moncur and Martin gave notice of a concrete interest, they were able to capitalise on Mackay's lifelong affection for Hearts as well as the personal circumstances that persuaded the player to stay in Edinburgh. Mackay joined at the same time as John Robertson, David Bowman and Ian Westwater – who were all schoolboy internationalists sought after by top English clubs – and though dark days were ahead of the club in the short term, the arrival of such youthful excellence was to play a major part in the long-term revival.

The dearth of talent at Tynecastle meant that Gary Mackay didn't have long to wait for his debut, coming on as a substitute against Ayr United, when Robert Connor and Steve Nicol were in their ranks, at Somerset Park in September 1980. Mackay appreciated that his chance arrived early because the team was struggling rather than through any extraordinary development on his part. Indeed, Mackay recalled finding the transition from juvenile football to reserve football less daunting than he did the step-up from the reserves to first-team action.

A slightly built young man who was not to gain extra strength and superior fitness until later in his career, Mackay struggled to catch the pace of first-team football in his early days. The physical strength required to operate as an out-and-out midfield player was also a burden on a lad of Mackay's tender years, and the player remembers that in his first Scottish Cup tie against Morton he was used in a role wide on the right and found that brief easier to handle.

Changes in the boardroom with the arrival of Wallace Mercer as chairman and the installation of a revolving door to the manager's office until Alex MacDonald was appointed as player-coach did not make for a stable playing environment in Mackay's early days. However, the teenager was not slow to spot the change in professional outlook that was brought to Tynecastle by the new broom, both on and off the field. Mackay remembered that when he first joined Hearts the playing squad were an amiable crowd but lacking in professionalism. This was summed up by the entrepreneurial ambition of one of the squad who used to sell Mars bars and cans of Coke to the rest of the players after training sessions and make a profit of two pence on each sale!

Alex MacDonald's promotion helped to put the playing side at Tynecastle on an even keel. Mackay believes that MacDonald knew only too well how much work needed to be done to turn the club around, but as a budding manager he at least had the consolation of only being able to take the club in one direction. As a pupil of the Jock Wallace school of excellence, MacDonald came to Hearts with an absolute conviction of the value of hard graft, and soon communicated to Mackay and his colleagues the need to roll the sleeves up. Mackay admits now that it took him a little longer than some others to get it into his head that fitness was as important as footballing ability. But once the penny dropped his improvement was rapid.

Mackay can recall how players of ability who were not prepared to buckle down and work at Tynecastle were shown the door. Individuals were always given a chance, but if they didn't want to take it, then they soon realised they had no place in Hearts' scheme of things.

Mackay is full of praise for the way MacDonald and Sandy Jardine, without being able to brandish the big cheque book, have bought wisely and gradually improved the quality of the playing staff. He thinks players have been signed on the basis of being willing to give it their best shot week in, week out, and individuals who might not have expected a career with a club of Hearts' calibre have grabbed their chance. Mackay believes it is exactly because MacDonald and Jardine have shown faith in people that the players have responded in kind by working hard to match the example set by the management team.

A member of the Scotland Youth team that won the European Championships in 1983, Mackay emerged as a regular selection in Andy Roxburgh's international squads during the 1987/88 season. When Craig Levein suffered a recurrence of a serious knee injury, Mackay succeeded him as team captain. He is a gregarious, likeable young man with a vigorous enthusiasm for football. Here, in his own words, Gary Mackay gives a unique insight into the life of a professional player in a diary account of a typical week with club and country.

SUNDAY: For a footballer this can be a wasted day. Everyone knows that on a Saturday night players go out and enjoy themselves. I find that if I get up around 11 and go to do some work with George McNeill, the sprint coach, at Meadowbank, it sets me up for the rest of the day and the rest of the week. It also helps me feel that I'm putting my time to good use.

If I do decide to go to Meadowbank, I'll normally do a good warm-up routine with the athletes who work with George. Then I might feel that I could do with a bit of running, but I prefer to work with the speedball and build up a sweat. When you've had a few lagers the night before, I find that the sooner you can get them out of your system the better. It is a mental thing as well as a physical one. For me, I feel better in my own mind getting up and doing something worth while.

On a Sunday afternoon there's often live football on television in England, and together with three or four friends I'll travel down to Coldingham and watch the match. It helps to break the day up, and I enjoy seeing games from south of the border because of the size of the crowds that attend the big matches and create a real atmosphere. The friends I go with will probably look at the game differently from the way I do. I want to look at individual players like Peter Reid of Everton and Bryan Robson of Manchester United and see if there are any little things I can pick up.

Since we are invariably involved in playing twice a week, there isn't much of a chance for me to watch football other than on a Sunday, and I don't think it does me any harm to keep up to date with the English scene, because in life you never know what can be waiting round the corner. I think it is important to be aware of what's happening in England and know a little about the style of play and the systems the teams use. If someone did come in for you in the future you would need to know if the club suited you.

In an international week, should Andy Roxburgh have picked me for a squad, my day will be different. Instead of getting up and going to Meadowbank, I'll have a lie-in and enjoy a quiet time at home. I'll travel through to Glasgow in the afternoon and then the squad moves down to Langbank and Gleddoch House Hotel. It is a terrific venue because it is so quiet. And when you are playing two games a week that is so important. The players are happy not to be in one of the bigger hotels with all the hustle and bustle of everyday life. The treatment we get at Gleddoch House is very individual and you can mix with the other players more easily. Hearts have also used the hotel before big games in the West of Scotland because it helps to keep everyone in a close environment. There are lots of activities available if that's what you want, and on the other hand there's the chance to relax.

MONDAY: Normally, after a Saturday game when the club have a fixture on the Wednesday, we're expected to come into Tynecastle around 11 although most of the players are in at the back of ten. The management take the view that rest is a vital part of a footballer's preparation, and there's the chance of a lie-in on a Monday.

There is no formal inquest into the Saturday game, and what you'll find is that the players talk about the match informally and give each other a bit of stick about what happened. We have a players' lounge that everyone meets in and the importance of that place in the story of

Hearts' improved fortunes shouldn't be underestimated. Mary, the tea lady, is one of the most important people at the club for the players, and the lounge is the most important place. In the past players used to rush in and rush away again from the ground. Now we can all get together in the players' lounge, and whether it was something on the television the night before or a game you've watched, then you're picking each other's brains and enjoying a good crack. When you just had the dressing-room to change in you found that players came in, did their work and went away again. Today players stay on till two if they want to do a bit extra and know they can go into the lounge and relax afterwards and have their lunch.

The only time the manager will speak to us directly about Saturday's game is if we've had a nightmare run for three or four weeks. Thankfully, that doesn't happen very often, and even a one-off bad experience is unlikely to result in a post-mortem. The manager takes the view that it is better to get a bad game out of your system, and on a Monday he's more likely to be up than down and that helps to get you in the right frame of mind for the next game on the Wednesday.

The work we do in training on a Monday is usually just a warm-up, though those who feel they need a bit extra can go down to Roseburn with the reserves and put in some additional work on shooting and crossing. But the manager prefers to keep everyone together at the warm-up, and normally there's a head tennis challenge afterwards with a £1 stake going to the winner. As far as the manager is concerned, I think that the head tennis is the top game of the week!

Seriously, in that context, he can talk to individuals and maybe give them a little stick about their touch on the Saturday or if their heading has left something to be desired. It might all look light-hearted, but the manager gets his point across in a different way. Instead of slagging a player, he'll let you know in his own fashion what was missing from your performance.

The routine with the international team on a Monday is different, obviously. There's more direct communication between Andy Roxburgh and the players. Given that we don't spend anything like as much time together, there's a need to discuss what happened last time. We'll have a fairly light training session and then you'll have a meeting to talk about your opponents and how the match differs from your previous game. The manager will also go through three or four routines in preparation for the international on the Wednesday. This is quite different from what happens at Tynecastle, where we won't know the team until a couple of hours before the kick-off. The international manager has a different job to do, and you'll have an idea on the Monday of what's likely to happen, though the team won't be confirmed until the following day.

When the international team plays abroad, I find that on the first night's stay in the hotel I tend to toss and turn and not sleep as well as I would do normally. The second night is usually no problem, however. You've adjusted to a new environment and are better placed to get that important rest before the game on the Wednesday. Foreign travel is very much a part of the modern footballer's life, and I don't think anyone could complain about the arrangements made for the international team, where you are always treated to the best of facilities. The players that moan can only do so for the sake of moaning. For me, the experiences abroad with the international team help to further your knowledge of the game. Those who complain maybe don't have the required enthusiasm for football.

Perhaps, having started my career with Hearts in the First Division, I'm more appreciative of any level of success than some others who started at the top. When you know what it is like to go to places like Alloa and change four at a time, it helps to keep things in perspective later on. There's no doubt it was good for me to enjoy a career where the direction was always moving up the way.

TUESDAY: This is the day, particularly when we don't have a mid-week fixture, that the players put in the hard work in training. It is our time for running and working out in the gym. We wouldn't expect to see a ball today, though when you are playing Saturday-Wednesday-Saturday there would be a lighter session every second Tuesday.

George McNeill and Bert Logan, the sprint coaches, come to Tynecastle on a Tuesday and work out with us on our fitness. The Hearts players have set themselves a high standard thanks to the help of George and Bert, who have shown us things that would not otherwise have been thought of. I know from a personal angle that I've had a pay-off from putting in the extra work. They are always available for us either individually or as a group, which is most helpful. I know that Pilmar Smith once helped George as a professional athlete to run in Australia, and maybe he feels that the work he does with us is like paying something back.

George and Bert are both characters who enjoy a laugh, and they know that if the players are genuinely putting the work in, then a bit of relaxation doesn't go amiss. That's a big part of the way it goes at Tynecastle – you work hard, but you also enjoy your work. There have even been times when George has brought the *Rocky* tapes into the gym when we've been hitting the speedball. The only thing is, he has to slow the music down, because some of us can't keep up with the rhythm!

From a personal point of view, there was a time around six or seven years ago when I regarded training as a bind and wasn't able to see how it could make me a better footballer. George and Bert explained that in the athletics world, if you've got the same ability to run as someone else, it is the guy who works harder who is going to come out on top. The same thing, I think, is true in football. If you take two players with the same skills, it is the one who works harder on improving his passing and touch as well as his fitness that will go that bit further in the game. It is an important realisation that in order to make the most of your ability, you've got to harness it with hard work.

With the Scotland squad on a Tuesday, we would do a lot of shadow exercises. That means when the manager names the side that is going to play the following night, the starting 11 will put the bibs on and play the other seven in the pool plus the trainers and whoever. It is their job to mimic the play of the side you are going to meet. This is so you can get an idea of how the other team are going to set themselves up against you.

These exercises are valuable for the players, because it could have been months since they last played together as a unit. It is a chance to get involved as a team and reacquaint yourself with the strengths and weaknesses of the players around you. Scotland would like to come close to reproducing the atmosphere of one of the top club sides, and having a captain like Roy Aitken is a big help in that respect. He's almost a father figure to the younger lads who have come in. Roy likes a joke, but it is hard work that has brought him success, and he's a good example to the rest that if you apply yourself you can go the right way.

WEDNESDAY: When we've got a game on the Wednesday night, I like a lie-in in the morning and will eat very little, just a light lunch at home. If it is a home game, then we are asked to report to Tynecastle at 3.15 p.m. What we do then is to go through a warm-up routine and then work on our free kicks and corners. It is at this point, usually around 4 p.m., that the team is named. We'll concentrate on our own set-pieces and also get an idea of what to expect from our opponents. But the managers don't dwell on the opposition too much. Basically it is down to what we do ourselves, and if we play to our capabilities we should win the game. There's no side nowadays that we need fear. Also, in the Premier Division, you meet other teams so often that they're unlikely to come up with anything that will surprise you.

It is different, of course, at international level, where your opponents are completely fresh to you. There are a lot of video sessions when you are away with the Scotland squad that help you to prepare. Some of the older professionals, although I'm not saying they don't find these sessions worth while, have been in the game that bit longer and can find the briefings a bit much. But for the younger, less experienced players, the video sessions can be of assistance in helping you to pick up snippets of information.

There's a huge difference between club football and international standards. Players rarely give the ball away needlessly in an international context. Different criteria can apply in League football. Playing at home when the crowd are urging you on, you find that players will put the ball into the box when perhaps they shouldn't. At international level, though, possession is so important − because the opposition will have a team of good players and if you let them have the ball it might be long enough before they let you have it back.

At Tynecastle, when half-time comes around we go through a ritual no matter how the game is progressing. Sandy Jardine appreciates that even if you are winning you have to keep the impetus going and maintain your advantage. On the other hand, should we be getting beaten, it is just a case of being patient. Of course, if you are not playing well then you will get your backside kicked. In my book that's part of the game. When you are only playing two games a week you are obliged to give those matches your best shot. Everybody knows that in order to maintain the progress that's been made at Tynecastle you've got to keep up the hard work. In that sense everyone's job is still on the line.

While our managers will pinpoint any individual flaws, they know that the team has been picked to do a job, and won't as a rule make hasty changes. You'll get the chance to play yourselves out of a bad patch.

After the game on a Wednesday night we've got the licence to go out and have a few beers. Alex and Sandy have always made the point that we should go out if we want to, but that we should not lose sight of the fact that the club will have a game on the Saturday. All the players at Tynecastle are good professionals, and if they're going to have a couple of drinks, they'll know the limit that is right for them.

THURSDAY: The players at Tynecastle never get a day off on a Thursday. The routine after a Wednesday night match is not dissimilar to what we do on a Monday. I would have a lie-in, and if it was a very physical match the night before, the warm-up will be short and sweet, followed by a long soak in a Radox bath. Again, there are no official inquiries into the events of the previous 90 minutes. We all get together and either get out of our system what's gone wrong or else try to build on what went right.

Outwith the training and the preparation for matches, a big part of your job as a footballer is your involvement with the community, both through supporters' clubs and charity work. As far as Hearts' first-team squad is concerned, only five of us live in Edinburgh, so you find that a lot of your time outwith playing the game is taken up on club-related business. There are bound to be occasions when you have to say 'no' to people because, like everyone else, footballers need time for themselves. I'm a talkative kind of person, and since that's my nature I find that I'm the one that gets asked to do a lot of things. I don't mind that. I like to think that I'm trying to put something back in for all the help that I've had in my career. I can look back to what Erich Schaedler and George Stewart used to do for Salvesens that helped my career. So any charity work, or helping kids or visiting hospitals, is just giving a little back in return.

Footballers are in the public eye, and as long as you don't get carried away with yourself it can be rewarding to try and put something into other people's lives. If possible, though, I like to keep Thursdays and Fridays for myself in order to relax. People have to come and go with you, and if it is not convenient to do something one night, you offer them an alternative date. But I appreciate that the club's involvement in the community is an important part of a footballer's responsibilities.

And, from your own point of view, there's always the goal of a testimonial year for the one-club player. Maybe the more you help others, the more you might help yourself in the long run. My present contract with Hearts will take me to ten years at Tynecastle, and you hope that loyalty will find its own reward.

Outwith football, my family have a pub in town that is run by my mum and dad. They look after the business 100 per cent and I don't get involved in that side of things behind the bar. But there are times when I've got a spare hour in the afternoon and I'll pop down and see the regulars.

FRIDAY: Today we'll normally go down to Roseburn after doing a bit of warm-up and get a touch of the ball. When you've had a match on the Wednesday you're only seeing the ball in game situations, and so a five-a-side match can help to put a bit of a competitive edge into your preparation. Not that there's any serious physical contact in these training matches. Everyone realises that it is far too close to the game on

Saturday to risk suffering an injury. But the work with the ball helps you to get your eye in and get the tools of the trade ticking over again.

When you are fulfilling a busy playing schedule, particularly in a physical league like the Premier Division, you are bound to pick up knocks in the course of a season. If I've got a minor injury I'll go and see our physiotherapist, Alan Rae. He's first-class at his job and you can visit him at the Royal Infirmary during the day when you're in need of urgent treatment, or else at his home at night, which can be more convenient for those of us who live locally.

The facilities at Tynecastle are good, and Alan can set out a programme of exercises and treatment for a player at the ground. After you've seen the physio and he's told you to rest, Alex and Sandy know that you won't lose your level of fitness in 48 hours. The rest is as important a part of the recovery process as any. There can even be times when you will be told not to go dancing on a Saturday night after the game! It might sound daft, but if you've picked up a knock in a match the last thing you need to do is aggravate it by going dancing. It is up to yourself how you react to things like that. Yet should you go to the dance, you might end up missing the game the following Wednesday. My feeling would be that there will be other times to go dancing, but there won't always be the opportunity to pick up the appearance money the following mid-week.

SATURDAY: When we are playing away from home, say in either Dundee or Glasgow, most of us will report to Tynecastle about 11 in the morning to get the bus. If the game is in the west, then we'll maybe pick up some of the players on the road through. Then we go for a bite to eat at one of the hotels in Glasgow. The same will happen when we go to Dundee. The lunch is a light one, and the important thing about the occasion is getting everyone together in a group. We'll watch the football programmes on BBC and ITV, when there are always little bits and pieces that you can pick up. We'll also have a few laughs, and that helps to get the banter going.

The professionalism of the club is such now that even what we eat is monitored. Years ago, when we went for a meal before the match, I would usually have a steak. Apparently it takes your system seven hours to digest a steak, so if you eat one at lunch-time you're not going to have digested it properly by match-time. The manager believes in the importance of diet, and he knew that was wrong. So steak is off the menu unless the physio has recommended it for you, and the players will sit down to chicken or fish or scrambled egg.

Unless we've done a training session at Tynecastle in the morning, we won't know the team until an hour or so before the kick-off. If we're going to Brockville in Falkirk, or Easter Road in Edinburgh, or even Motherwell, we'll have a short session at Tynecastle. But when you're facing a longer bus drive to the match you don't want to be sitting in an enclosed space after training. That's when you could find yourself tightening up.

As for the game itself, as a professional you have to try and go through your performance afterwards and analyse it. Other people will give you some ideas of what's happened, and if the management have a go at you after the game, you need to realise that it is not a personal thing. It is the simple fact that things have not gone as well as they should have done on the day for the team. These are aspects of the game you have to learn from.

Yet there are also games where it is better afterwards to just block things out of your mind. When your own form is good, you can even block out a couple of mistakes during the match itself. Otherwise, notably when you are going through a bad spell, a couple of mistakes will get it into your head that whatever you do next will also be a bad mistake. That's why confidence and maturity are such important assets for a player. You have to be able to say, well, I'm just going to get on with it and do something constructive the next time. No matter what anyone says, the biggest factor in football is self-belief. The player who is convinced that he's better than the guy he's playing against will always do well.

When your mind is settled, that also helps. There's no doubt that when a player is coming to the end of his contract with a club and is wondering whether anyone will come in for him or should he stay where he is, that can have an effect on form. In early 1987, when my contract was up for renewal, I think I let myself go mentally and allowed some things to get me down. When I did sign a new contract with the club in the summer it was a good deal for me, given the way I had been playing. At the end of the day you've got to fire the bullets to get the pay-off. If my contract was up for renewal now it might be a different story. But I also appreciate that maintaining my present form can only improve my situation the next time my contract runs out.

What I understand more fully than before is that the 90 minutes on a Wednesday or a Saturday are the most important things in a footballer's life. If there are worries in the background, and footballers are just like everyone else in that respect, you just have to try and black them out.

On a Saturday night I'll always try and go into the bar for the first hour and speak to some of the regulars. It isn't always possible when there are supporters' functions, but otherwise I'll talk to a group of lads who come in after the game and hear their ideas on the match. Sometimes it can go in one ear and out the other because you've not got your mind settled about what's happened. There's a group I sit with every week and we always have a discussion about the match. The lads are very knowledgeable and have watched the club for a number of years. They know what they're on about, though from my point of view you do have to pick and choose who you sit with. The last thing you want is someone being a pain in the neck and giving you a hard time.

Afterwards I'll usually go out. Saturday night is the traditional night to have a few drinks and relax. It is important to unwind, and I can remember when Andy Roxburgh was in charge of the Scotland Youth team in Finland and we qualified for the final of the European Championships, three days beforehand Andy and Walter Smith took all the players down to the bar and gave us four lagers each. We knew we'd achieved something and were on a high. Having a couple of drinks was the best thing for us, and I remember going to bed and enjoying a terrific sleep. Looking back, I think that made a difference to our approach in the final. We had wound down and relaxed, and were then able to go on to the next stage of winning the tournament. At home, letting your hair down on a Saturday night helps to set you up for the week to come.

CHAPTER ELEVEN

The Sweeper

MIKE AITKEN

I F ASKED to compare his role at Tynecastle with a position on the field of play Les Porteous, the club secretary, suggested that he might be described as a sweeper. He's a type who mops up the bits and piece, plugs gaps left by others and tries to ensure that the back-up is available for the midfield general in the boardroom and the ball-winners in the manager's office to run the game to Hearts' best advantage.

In many respects the secretary is the eyes and ears of a club. The key figure in a compact staff of nine who administer the business of Hearts on a day-to-day basis – on match days anything up to 200 people will be involved in some capacity or other – Les Porteous has the confidence of everyone from the chairman to the groundsman. He describes himself as a good listener and believes that quality to be a valuable asset. In short, he knows when to talk and when to say nothing. A man with a loose tongue, it seems, would not be the most suitable candidate for a job in which a knowledge of the ever-thickening books of rules and regulations never matters more than a large helping of common sense.

A former employee of the National Coal Board at Newtongrange and Monktonhall – he worked there for 16 years after leaving school – Porteous was a keen teenage footballer. The advice of a shrewd father, however, convinced him that even if he trained and practised until the onset of middle age he would still not be good enough to make the grade.

Having lost interest in the playing side, Porteous began to pay attention to the running of the local Junior club, Newtongrange Star, and stood for election to the committee. "I didn't want to find myself without an involvement in football," he recalled. "There were half a dozen of us who took up with Newtongrange at that point, and I was their representative at meetings and became one of the youngest-ever life members of the East of Scotland Football Association."

Chairman of the Fife and Lothians Junior Football Association, Porteous was immersed in the administration of the game from a tender age. The prospect of making his living from football, however, never crossed his mind. "I didn't work as hard at school as I know I should have done. After I got a summer job I decided that I could achieve more in life than my limited qualifications would allow me to do at that point. There were so many hurdles in my way that I went to night school and day release. The Coal Board did me a real turn because they forced me to pursue qualifications in business studies and at the Institute of Personnel Management that I might not otherwise have been in a position to take."

When a successor was sought to Jim Calder as secretary of Hearts in 1980 Porteous, who had grown restless as an ambitious young man unable to secure promotion in what was a contracting coal industry, felt that an application could lose him nothing: "I'd begun to look elsewhere for employment, and when the job at Tynecastle came up I thought I'd try for it. I was interested in football, had some administrative experience and was a dyed-in-the-wool Hearts supporter. But, in all honesty, I regarded my chances of getting the post as rather less than slim."

Before Archie Martin became involved as chairman, Hearts were a club in decline, without even a full-time secretary to administer their affairs. The arrival of Martin heralded a time of change, with the club's constitution being opened up to attract the kind of funding that Wallace Mercer was to bring to Tynecastle. Having secured the post of secretary, Porteous found himself very much thrown in at the deep end.

"Within six months I was hurled into a rights issue, and I wasn't even sure if I could spell it, never mind organise one. I ended up working anything from 12 to 14 hours a day because a deadline had been set and no provision was made for administration. The directors themselves were not quite sure of what was involved, and while the registration was handled by the registrars office at the Bank of Scotland, all the original letters to shareholders and the matching up of allocations on a two-to-one basis was done from my desk," he recalled.

Involved from the very beginning in the new broom that was to sweep away the cobwebs of recession, Porteous found the turmoil of those early days a benefit to his career rather than a hindrance. "I learned more in three years than I could have done in a lifetime of training. It was a gamble for me to come here in the sense that I was giving up a secure post. As a family, we thought long and hard about it, and took a holiday before eventually coming to a decision. It was my wife who said, 'If you don't take the chance, you'll regret it all your life'.

"Funnily enough, there's an old chap at Newtongrange who took the treasurer's job on a temporary basis 45 years ago and has still got it. He passed on the advice to me that it was the same figures, only bigger. At first I couldn't see what he meant. And truly the biggest mistake I made in my first 18 months in the job was to hold the belief that everyone knew better than me. I'm not trying to beat my own drum here, but it took me a while to appreciate that the needs of a fully professional football team are the same as any others. The only difference is that for the players their employment depends on how they play the game. As I'd been told, everything else is the same, only bigger and a bit more complicated," said Porteous.

Eight years into his career with Hearts. Porteous believes he has a valid contribution to make, but has never lost a sense of humility or humour. "There is a danger for people who stay in this job long-term that they begin to think the club can't work without them. That's nonsense, of course. You must never be beguiled into thinking it would cause any hiccups if you weren't around," he said.

The duties and responsibilities of a club secretary in the 1980s have become ever more complex. A club's involvement with its own supporters, with the community, with other clubs and the football authorities is governed by more paperwork than ever before. The days when a club could just open its doors and play a match without giving much thought to anything other than the quality of the team are long gone.

As far as Hearts' relationship with the club's fans is concerned, Porteous is an enthusiastic devotee of the open-door policy initiated by Wallace Mercer. This applies to employees of the club as well as outsiders. "There used to be a terrible situation under previous régimes where no one was allowed beyond the door at the reception area except the directors. I can remember a player being put out for no good reason other than it had been decided that he had no right to be there. When that was the attitude towards the players you can imagine why the supporters were kept at arm's length," he said.

The appointment of John Frame to liaise between the club and the supporters and an acknowledgement on Hearts' behalf that more was required than the cavalier attitude of previous administrations brought a fresh affinity to what had previously been a "them and us" situation. "I think you can trace the improvement in the behaviour of the Hearts fans to the time when they began to feel that they had some input into the running of things. The way the federation of supporters clubs has mushroomed over the years also indicates that the fans feel they are being fairly treated," he added. When chairman Wallace Mercer held a dinner attended by a group of representatives from the federation of supporters clubs, both sides felt they were on the same wavelength. "The biggest problem facing Hearts when I started work here was the 'them and us' attitude that divided the club from its support. Having been brought up in a mining community I wasn't used to approaching life in that way. The open-door policy has done more than anything else to erase that difficulty," said Porteous.

As far as Hearts' relationship with the Scottish League and the SFA is concerned, the Tynecastle secretary doesn't pretend to know the rule books off by heart (he thinks that only the doyen of club secretaries, the late Desmond White of Celtic, could quote pages from memory), but he has learned how to tread a safe path through the minefield of regulations that dictate the circumstances under which a club can conduct its business. "It is all about experience, and I would defy anyone to tell me that they could master the job without building up knowledge from year to year. If you make a slight mistake it sticks in your mind and you know better than to repeat the blunder should a similar set of circumstances arise again."

One of the areas that has become increasingly sensitive in recent times is the renewal of a player's contract, and for the secretary there is the onerous responsibility of not making a costly gaffe. "The slightest mistake, a wrong comma or a full stop, and a player who could have a transfer value in excess of £750,000 would be entitled to a free transfer. It is a state of affairs that concentrates the mind wonderfully," he revealed.

Porteous cannot envisage a time in the immediate future when a player's entitlement to freedom of movement will put an end to the transfer market. He thinks there will always have to be some form of compensation for the club that is left behind, or else the structure of the game as we know it would be put at risk. "Times have changed in football since the days when the club held the whip hand. Now it is the players who have the edge in negotiations. Any player who doesn't seek an advantageous contract is a fool. It never crosses the minds of young men that they could suffer an injury that would put them out of football. But these things happen, and players have to be aware of the bigger picture than just what happens on a week-to-week basis. It makes sense for the individual to try and get himself a long-term contract that adds a little bit of security. Getting the balance set correctly between the rights of the employers and the rights of the employees is always tricky, but in football at present the advantage rests with the players," Porteous observed.

The Hearts secretary draws up the contract for a new player once the club and the individual have agreed terms. Porteous works on the basis that it is to everyone's advantage that the document is kept as simple as possible. There will be references to the basic wage, appearance money and an attachment indicating that the level of bonuses will be agreed between the management and the staff. Hearts tend not to specify other financial considerations in their contracts, and future deals with players are left unhindered by a general summing up that usually indicates terms will be no less favourable than in the previous contract. Having said that, however, what Hearts promise a new player is what that new player will receive. "In Wallace Mercer's time here as chairman there's been an honesty and a straightforwardness in dealing with the players. And if there's been any element of doubt regarding a contract, he's come down on the side of the players."

The average player will usually make his living at a club from four main sources of income – the inducement to sign, the basic wage, appearance money and bonuses for points. The inducement to sign can cover a number of financial aspects including either a signing-on fee or an interest-free loan. This is particularly helpful when a player moves from a part of the country where house prices are low to a city like Edinburgh where there is a booming property market.

While a number of loopholes regarding payments to footballers were closed by the Inland Revenue after a spring amnesty, many players benefited from Nigel Lawson's tax cuts. At Tynecastle, for instance, a regular first-team member could expect to earn, bonuses included, around £30,000 a year, while a star turn could make as much as £50,000. For these individuals the cuts in the higher bands of taxation were certainly good news.

Of course, Hearts have been shrewd enough to appreciate that the more a player earns, the higher his value if and when he comes out of contract and chooses to leave. When a player opts to move to the Continent it is his age, his status and his salary, which is multiplied by a factor of ten, that decide the size of the fee.

The club's dealings with Europe are not just restricted to the transfer market, of course. An involvement in one of the three European club competitions can present a number of headaches for a club secretary in the course of making arrangements for a large travelling support. When Hearts drew Paris St Germain in the UEFA Cup they were advised by the SFA not to take any tickets at all for the away leg of the tie.

"Our attitude was that if the situation was handled properly, there was no reason why we shouldn't take 5,000 supporters with us. I went to Paris and met the secretary of the French opponents and asked him if he would ensure that we were the only selling agency for tickets for Hearts supporters. We made people go through the procedure of bringing a passport in when they came to buy a ticket, and noted how they planned to travel and where they were staying. We then gave a list of names to the transport police, who knew exactly how many Hearts supporters were travelling on which days.

"We also contacted the police in Paris, and after the match we received a letter from the Mayor telling us that everything had gone off in a trouble-free manner. In spite of the dire warnings before the tie, Hearts' supporters were good ambassadors for their club as well as the game in Scotland. That situation backed up my belief that, with all due respect to the media, it is not enough just to make announcements that you want people to behave. You've got to get them in and let them know exactly what you want. And once you've invited them to fill in the forms, that has the same deterrent effect as the use of video cameras in the ground. Having said all that, you've got to take each situation as it comes. For instance, if we were to draw a club from Holland, we would want to look closely at the circumstances before encouraging our supporters to travel."

As far as security is concerned on the domestic front, Hearts have put in a lot of effort over the past eight years in recruiting their own team of stewards. "We employ the same number of stewards for every game, regardless of whether Rangers or Motherwell are the visitors. It is important to secure their loyalty. There are more then 100 stewards at Tynecastle on match days, and we know they've been through fire training, emergency procedure training and are well qualified to cope with crowd control. Our stewards have a good reputation and were called upon at the Commonwealth Games as well as at Murrayfield and for concerts.

"Apart from our well-trained stewards, we use video cameras and have installed stout fencing. Overall, we've taken all the precautions that we can to ensure the safety of the crowd. Ever since the disaster at

Bradford, it is necessary to have a working knowledge of the safety of your ground. There are aspects to be considered like the strength of the concrete, testing of crash barriers and metal testing that have to be dealt with in order to maintain a valid safety certificate. In European competitions there are a host of additional regulations. They even want to know the strength of your floodlights in relation to the size of your ground!"

Like many football grounds built in a different age, Tynecastle, which had a capacity of over 53,000 in the 1930s, is now limited to a gate of almost half that that number. Consequently, Hearts are always searching the trade papers for any available land adjacent to the stadium. "Even a small strip of land 15 to 20 feet wide could help us to increase our capacity by as many as 4,000 spectators," said Porteous. "It is not that we even need the space, because there is plenty of room on the terracings. But regulations regarding the number of exits are strict. I think, when you are talking about getting out of a stand, which is an enclosed structure and vulnerable to fire, that's fair enough. But there are a limited number of things that can happen on an uncovered terracing. If your crash barriers are up to the mark – and ours have been tested to take 1.8 tons – there shouldn't be too many problems."

It is clear that in the 1980s the secretary of a sizeable football club needs to be something of a renaissance man with a knowledge ranging from crowd control, to building engineering, to the intricacies of the penalty points system imposed by the Scottish Football Association's disciplinary committee. Tommy Walker, who ran Hearts in the 1950s throughout their most successful era, told Les Porteous on his appointment that he would enjoy his post but that the job of administering a football club was bound to become trickier rather than more straightforward, even if the basics of the job remained the same. "There has been a dramatic increase in paperwork to carry out ultimately the same functions," Porteous observed. As a jack-of-all-trades, the club secretary takes an interest in virtually every aspect of the running of the club. "The commercial department is the one that probably involves me least of all. But even there Charles Burnett, our commercial manager, will drop by for a chat and tell me about things that could involve me."

Given this participation in so many different areas, the secretary is in a unique position to look at an idea from someone else's angle. "It is a privileged role. You can act as a cartilage between different points of view. Maybe I can help people to see what sort of effect a particular line of thinking could have on the administration of the club. A lot of people in the club come to me with what they think are good ideas, and you point out certain things to them. The phrase or expression I hear most is, 'I never thought of that'. Then the person concerned goes away, revamps his thinking and comes back with the right thing.

Ground improvements are taking place all the time at Tynecastle – these are the latest turnstiles at the McLeod Street end of the ground.

"I don't consider myself an ideas man. I'm more the practical type. I can say, 'Well, we can go down that road but it will have an effect on this, an effect on that, and we'll need to change a variety of things to see it through'. That's my way of doing things, and I think as a club secretary you have to be available. Perhaps there are other secretaries who prefer to isolate themselves from other aspects of club life. It isn't my way of doing things. And, to be honest, I don't think you can do the job properly any other way.

"I know exactly how far I can go with taking everyday decisions on my own without referring to the chairman first. Basically, my job is to carry out and interpret the decisions taken by the executive on a daily basis. When I make a mistake I'm the first to admit it, because no one can get it right all the time. Someone once said that in management if you get 51 decisions out of 100 right you're a genius. But if you only get 49 right, then you'll be branded as a madman. When you do go wrong, the important thing is to learn from the mistake and not repeat it.

"What I enjoy most about my job is that I can honestly say there's never been a day when I didn't look forward to walking through the main door. Even when times were rough I always wanted to get in here and do something. What has always been clear to me is that if the club have good players, then everything else will fall into place. When the football is worth watching, then the supporters will turn out regardless. When it isn't, it doesn't matter how marvellous your administration is or how terrific your facilities are the supporters will stay away. The team is the key to everything."

CHAPTER TWELVE

Labour of Love

MIKE AITKEN

IN THE FAMILY of Hearts, there are numerous people behind the scenes unknown to the public who make a valuable contribution to the running of the club. Many of these individuals are unpaid as well as unsung, though it goes without saying that in frequent instances Hearts would not be the same without their services.

The management team of Alex MacDonald and Sandy Jardine both enjoyed prolonged careers as players themselves, and from the beginning of their time in charge at Tynecastle held the opinion that a grounding in high-powered fitness was just as important in the preparation of the modern footballer as skill or temperament. MacDonald and Jardine wanted Hearts to enjoy a high standard of physical conditioning, and the fact that the Edinburgh side became one of the quickest and fittest teams in the Premier Division – a league that sets exacting standards of fitness – suggests they may not have been unsuccessful in their aim.

As a player in the early 1970s, Sandy Jardine had consulted Tom Paterson, the former Powderhall sprinter, about rebuilding his running action. Jardine became involved for a spell in professional sprinting, taking part in events throughout the Borders, winning races and improving the speed that was also to make him a more effective footballer. It was not uncommon at this time for footballers to take part in professional sprinting, though no one else emulated the success of George McNeill, who went from a playing career with Hibs and

Stirling Albion to winning the New Year's Day Sprint and making a name for himself as an exceptionally gifted sprinter. In a less hypocritical age, McNeill would have had medals to show for his talent by representing Scotland as an athlete. As it was, his training methods subsequently exerted a profound influence on the careers of others, and when his own involvement ended George McNeill was invited to apply some of the techniques that had helped sprinters to run faster to assist the playing staff at Tynecastle to improve their speed.

The only man ever to complete the double of Powderhall Sprint (1970) and the Stowell Easter Gift Sprint Handicap in Australia (1981), McNeill was still winning races at the age of 40. If anything, he was better known Down Under than he was anywhere in Scotland other than his home town of Tranent, and it was through the man who sponsored some of his trips to Australia, Edinburgh bookmaker and Tynecastle director Pilmar Smith, that George McNeill first became involved with Hearts.

"Pilmar and I had become good friends because of the Australian connection. He knew the methods that we used as athletes to improve our fitness, and took an interest in what we were doing from the athletics angle as well as the betting side. When Alex and Sandy took over at Hearts, Pilmar came to me and asked if I would like to get involved. It was something I was happy to do, and once I'd chatted to the Hearts management team I knew how convinced they were that we had something to offer them.

"I was more or less given a free hand to bring in our methods on the physical training side. I'd had an involvement with Hibs, Stirling Albion and Morton in my own playing days, and always held the opinion that footballers only achieved a fraction of their potential fitness in the upper body. As a sprinter I'd spent 16 or 17 years working for seven nights a week on my upper body and never experienced feelings of tiredness. My view was that footballers had not even begun to scratch the surface in this aspect of fitness. It used to be the case that when you saw a footballer stripped off he'd have strong legs and nothing up top. My feeling has always been that you are only as good as your weakest link. People think that in order to improve speed we only concentrated on giving players races over 30 yards. But that was only a very small part of the preparation. The big change we made was in the gymnasium training. That's where the players will punch the speedball and work the other circuits," he said.

Recalling his own days as a footballer, George McNeill could remember the prevailing thinking that 20 abdominal exercises were considered hard graft. Today a Hearts player will build up to eight sets of 50 abdominal exercises and 20 press-ups. As a consequence Hearts have become one of the fittest sides in the country. The success of the training programme, mark you, wasn't achieved overnight.

Pictured here with sprinter Linford Christie, sprint coach George McNeill has done marvellous work in training with the Hearts players.

"In the first year I said to Alex and Sandy that they should encourage a few of the players to come and see me during the close season. The thing about footballers is that when you have midweek games as well as Saturday matches, the need for rest periods and time to recuperate from injuries means that there is only one day a week when you can work the players hard. In order to build a bank of fitness that they can draw on the rest of the year round, I suggested that it would be worth while for some of the players to come and see me during the close season. People like John Robertson and Gary Mackay did do that, and when they came back the following year with a few others they'd raised their level that bit higher and were able to kick on to the next stage. What we're finding now is that apart from playing together for the past couple of years, the present Hearts team has also been training together and improved their strength and speed as a group. It is something that will continue to benefit the players throughout their careers. Our involvement won't make a footballer – that's all to do with touch and use of the ball – but we can help someone who already has those qualities and make them a stronger and faster athlete.

"I suppose a classic example would be Gary Mackay. He was a lad who was never strong in the tackle, but in those areas where he was lacking before he's gained a new dimension. What happens is that when a player begins to feel stronger and better within himself, then he's really keen to do the training. Players soon discover that they last the 90 minutes better and that no one shoves them about," he said.

McNeill takes the view that a much higher standard of fitness is required by the footballer of 1988 than was the case in 1968. He believes that state of affairs is only right and proper given the strides that have been made in other sports like athletics, where sprinters will train every night of the week without financial reward to spur their efforts.

"When I played football, the players who were involved in the first team looked upon training as a necessary evil. It was something they had to suffer in order to play on the Saturday. If there were days when they were let off to work on crosses then they were delighted. Things are different now, and while it used to be a fair criticism of full-time footballers that they behaved like part-time ones, today at a club like Hearts it is instilled in players when they sign how important fitness is and how hard they will have to work," he added.

McNeill has observed how various Hearts players have begun to regard a heavier training schedule as second nature. "Gary Mackay will even come and see me on a Sunday morning," he said. "The thing is that the exercise we use with the speedball can give the feeling of a command of a skill as well as just hard work."

Training a footballer, however, offers a different challenge from training a sprinter. McNeill explained the change in emphasis. "As far as football is concerned, we do more work regarding stamina. Football is an aerobic exercise in which players have to run for 90 minutes. Sprinters, on the other hand, are trained so that they can release their power over ten seconds. Because of that we've adapted our exercises. The running exercises have a shorter recovery period, and we probably give the footballers more quantity of exercises than for the pure sprinter. In the gym the work is pretty much the same. You are building up their strength, with particular emphasis on the upper body.

The thing is that footballers already get plenty of leg work as it is."

Footballers concentrate on sustained running during the pre-season period. When McNeill takes a training session with Hearts on a Tuesday during the football season itself, the emphasis is on short bursts of pace with subsequently short periods of recovery. This is in order to relate the training to the reality of what happens on the field of play.

McNeill has also worked on improving the running action of different players. "A lot of players think that because they're moving their legs and their arms quickly, then that means fast. But if you say to them 'Look, you could be moving at a slightly slower speed but covering much more ground', then they begin to learn how to beat an opponent. Technical things like that are important for a footballer, not so much when they've got the ball and need to use their arms for balance, but when they've not got it and are trying to make a run back. That's when economy of movement is so important, because you are running in a relaxed manner and not burning up your energy."

Another talent McNeill has been able to pass on from the sprinter's repertoire of skills to the footballers he works with is judgement of pace. "When you are sprinting in race situations you can start to assess the quickness of others. In football, if a player is running through on the ball and there's someone at his back chasing him, he'll know not to panic. Players can learn an awareness of how long it is going to take the other guy to catch up. In essence it is a question of gaining greater control of a situation."

McNeill understands that some men are born faster than others – there is such a thing as natural pace – and those who are slow off the mark are unlikely to ever become speed merchants. But the footballer with average pace can be made quicker. "Everyone has wondered for years why the speedball is a piece of equipment that seems to produce results for sprinters. Research was undertaken in this field in Australia, and they discovered that punching the speedball helped to tune up the fibre in the muscle that helps you to run faster: without wanting to get too technical on the subject, it is maybe enough to say that there is scientific evidence to prove why this form of training can increase speed," he said.

McNeill is quick to make the point that whatever the sound nature of the theories the training wouldn't have worked for Hearts if Alex MacDonald and Sandy Jardine had not given their full backing to the programme of preparation. "We were given every encouragement, and there was never any question of trying to make one speedball work for ten people. Everything is organised properly and the work is done to a pattern. Elsewhere, the system hasn't worked as well because the clubs have not followed the training programme so faithfully. It is not something you can toy with. When I first went to Tynecastle, I told them it had to be done this way or else it wasn't going to be any good. Alex and Sandy were both still playing at the time, and it probably helped that they were able to feel the benefits for themselves."

McNeill, even though he was pronounced *persona non grata* by amateur athletics throughout his career, is one of the finest sprinters Scotland has ever produced. He bears no grudges, but admits that his involvement with football now gives him more pleasure than coaching athletes. "Since my running career finished, my work with Hearts means more to me than the athletics. Because I signed for Hibs at 15, people think that's who I support – but when you work with people and you realise what a good club you are involved with, that's the most important thing by far.

"To be honest, I do it all for nothing. I wouldn't change that because I think I've got one of the luckiest positions in football. When I go on trips with Hearts I'll dine with Alex and Sandy. I attend nearly every players' night out. And on a Saturday I sit with the directors and Wallace Mercer always looks after me. So right throughout the club I've got a good relationship with everyone. My job's not at stake, which means there's no pressure on me. It is the kind of position that people in the executive club would pay thousands for!"

George McNeill regards Hearts as the best club in the country to work for, and similar feelings of respect and camaraderie lie behind the dedication of John Binnie, an accountant by profession, who in his spare time operates as Hearts' reserve team coach.

Binnie make no secret of the fact that his role at Tynecastle is a time-consuming one. He tries to get down to the ground each lunchtime in order to keep in touch with what's happening. His involvement at nights usually stretches from Monday to Thursday. On top of that little lot there's the Saturday match to take care of. Binnie does earn a small fee for his trouble, though like George McNeill cash is not the motivation for putting in long hours. "First and foremost, I enjoy doing the job. Of course it is demanding, and you find yourself away from home a fair bit. But when you get pleasure from doing something it doesn't feel like a chore. I suppose the situation has been more difficult for my family than for me," he said.

Formerly involved with Falkirk, and having spent a number of years at Brockville, John Binnie's involvement with Hearts came about through a telephone call from Sandy Jardine. "He got in touch with me one night and asked me if I would consider taking the reserves. Sandy made it clear that the club could only offer me pennies at the time. There was no guarantee of the financial situation improving, but as things have worked out the job has been great for me. Don't get me wrong, it is nice to get the cash that goes with the post but the financial thing is incidental. The money doesn't relate to the time you put in. I suppose you could describe it as a labour of love," he added.

When he was first involved with Hearts, the club had a number of part-time players on their books like Donald Park, Derek O'Connor, Brian McNaughton and Ian Westwater. In recent seasons at Tynecastle the emphasis has swung very much towards a full-time involvement, both with the reserves and the first-team squad. "My situation is that I take around a dozen lads on a Monday night. They are in the 15 to 16 age group and come from all over Scotland. What you are trying to achieve is to help these youngsters polish up on the basics and give them an understanding of the principles of the game. Basically the job is about teaching good habits. You want young players to go about their business in a disciplined manner. Even little things like the way they warm up are important. You want to get certain ways of doing things into their heads – and get them to think a little about how they approach the game," he said.

Like any other coach, John Binnie likes to see his players winning matches but harbours no illusions about the functions of a reserve side within the context of a leading club. "My feeling on this is that the reserves are there to bring on the young ones. Results are less important at the end of the day than the quality of the players that you bring through. As far as I'm concerned the bottom line is the progress that's been made day to day, week to week by the younger players."

Occupied as he is with helping to bring on the next generation of first-team players, Binnie holds the view that Scotland still produces a crop of top-quality players, though perhaps not the same quantity as before. "I think there is still an élite band of players in this country: the five per cent or so who are quite exceptional. I think the band below that, however, is not quite as broad as it was a number of years ago. To some extent, you are now looking at lads and saying, 'Well, he's got one or two possibilities; maybe we should take him. If we take a chance, then perhaps we can add to what he's got.' These days you've got to make the most of people's strengths.

"There's virtually no chance of a good young player going unnoticed now. Occasionally you will get the boy who loses his way slightly and comes again at a later date. You might call this type a sleeper. But generally speaking the Juvenile and Junior games are so well covered, as well as the First and Second Divisions, that there aren't many young players you don't know about."

Hearts cast their net wide in the search for promising youngsters and draw talent from Ayrshire, Glasgow and Stirling to John Binnie's Monday night training sessions. On a Thursday night, the coach puts local lads from the Lothian area through their paces.

Given the highly competitive nature of the Premier Division, fewer young players make an immediate breakthrough into first-team football than used to be the case. In this respect Hearts are no different from other clubs in their appreciation of experience. However, for the younger player waiting his chance in the reserves, patience as well as ambition is needed.

"There are many factors involved in whether or not a young lad can make the step up to first-team football. Can he handle it physically, for instance? Even if a boy has all the talent you might want, there's also the consistency factor to consider. Those who can run and have ability don't always produce. Under those circumstances a club with a strong first-team squad can afford to put a youngster back into the reserves, whereas a less well-off team might have no option but to persevere with the player.

"In the old days, at a club like Rangers a player could serve an apprenticeship of up to five years in the reserves. Then there was a period when, if you were not in the first team by the time you were 19, people thought you weren't going to make it. Now the situation has come full circle again and more maturity is required.

"Even players who have been with us for a number of years and haven't established themselves as first-team members could do a job for the club in the short term because their standards have come on by leaps and bounds. But when you look at the pressures on teams in the Premier Division, it isn't surprising that managers feel the need to bank on experience. With so much at stake it is hard for youngsters to break through – but you've got to give the good ones a taste of it or they won't have that incentive to spur them on.

"There is a difference between league football and the reserve scene. Of course the reserves mean different things to different people. For a new lad, everything is fresh and each Saturday brings a challenge. But once you've been doing it for a few years the challenge begins to tail off. That's why it is important for those you want to encourage to have the hope of being involved in a first-team pool or of going for a trip with the club.

"Reserve football does mean different things to different people. I'm not saying that players don't give it their best shot. But the adrenalin flows faster for some individuals than for others. We're fortunate at Tynecastle in that even those who come down from the first team have an excellent attitude. Of course that has a lot to do with the competitive approach of Alex MacDonald and Sandy Jardine, who won't tolerate sloppiness. They take part in things, and though there is a lot of laughing and joking about the place, when it is time to get down to work you would almost think someone had pulled a switch," he said.

John Binnie's admiration for Hearts' management team and their thorough involvement in all respects of the playing side is shared by Alan Rae, the club's physiotherapist, who also works at Tynecastle on a part-time basis. Having qualified as a physiotherapist in 1966 and worked overseas as well as for the health service, Rae thought he'd missed his chance of an involvement in football before meeting up with Sandy Jardine.

Injuries are part and parcel of the football scene and Hearts are fortunate to have a first-class physiotherapist in Alan Rae (right).

Alan Rae, who grew up in Dumfries, first met Jardine in the capital in 1978. Four years later, when the former Rangers player moved to Tynecastle to work with Alex MacDonald, Jardine contacted Rae through a mutual friend and asked him if he would work as a physiotherapist for the club. Rae, who is employed at the Royal Infirmary and also runs his own chartered physiotherapy practice, described the offer as a bolt from the blue.

When he first took up Hearts' offer the club had little or no spare cash, and Rae helped out on an *honorarium* basis. The physio, who was a frustrated footballer himself as a youngster, did believe, however, that Hearts were going places, and that it might not be long before better times returned to Tynecastle.

"When I came to Hearts in 1982 I don't think I'd been to their ground for at least 12 years. I'd been busy raising a family as well as working, and I'd got out of the habit of watching the game. But my home background was always football and, like every lad of my age, my ambition was to be a professional footballer. I was never good enough to achieve that ambition, though when I became a physiotherapist I was always interested in treating sports injuries. Luckily it wasn't until I was more experienced that my chance came along – and I think I'm better qualified to do the job now than when I first started. I'm sure I would have made more mistakes if I'd gone into it earlier.

"It is demanding to combine the work with Hearts with my other commitments, but I suppose I am always thinking in physiotherapy terms. It is a bit like being a reporter in the newspaper business – whether you are covering news or sport the same journalistic principles apply. The same goes in my line. You are always looking at things through a physiotherapist's eyes," he said.

In Rae's estimation, the treatment of sports injuries is a more complex and demanding field than ever before, simply because in football, for instance, the game has become faster and footballers are fitter than ever before. Paradoxically, the more sophisticated an athlete's body becomes, the more difficult it is to handle when it breaks down.

"You have to constantly remind players of the need for them to rest their bodies. Controlled rest and controlled exercise – with rest making up 70 per cent of the picture – are the key factors in helping someone to regain fitness. You do get people who are born athletes and who can be involved in sport for 14 years not picking up a serious injury. As a rule, the better the athlete the fewer injuries he is likely to pick up. An individual can be very fit, but nonetheless remain a poor natural athlete.

He is the type who will pick up more knocks and experience injury problems. The fortunate ones have a natural resilience. And even players who can look superb athletes may have a brittleness underneath which will see them encounter problems every four or five matches," he said.

Alan Rae defines the physiotherapist's role in a modern football club as being related to two important areas – assessment of injury and management of injury. "It is not always hands-on treatment or electrical treatment," he stressed. "The main thing is keeping the player right, giving him advice and directing him on how he should be conducting his recovery phase. The instances of sitting and getting short 15-minute bursts of treatment are only a minuscule part of the treatment programme. It might make a good picture for a newspaper, but far more important is the need to look at a player as an individual. You have to ask, 'Why is he breaking down? Is he feeding himself properly, is he sleeping long enough, is his home life harmonious?' All these factors come into it, though I would hasten to add I don't think of myself as either a psychologist or a psychiatrist!

"Players coming into full-time football can have a lot of cash as well as spare time on their hands, and you want to know if they are sitting down in front of the television in the afternoon and devouring a couple of pizzas out of boredom. In my opinion this is where Sandy Jardine and Alex MacDonald come into their own, because they give careful thought to a number of factors that most people would never dream of considering in the context of running a football team."

Like his colleagues in the medical profession, Alan Rae subscribes to the theory that prevention is better than cure. He takes the view that warm-up exercises and the preparation for intense physical effort are vital. "This was always an important area," he went on, "but nowadays, when people are more car-orientated and spend a lot of time sitting down watching television, there is a trend whereby players are less active outwith their work at the ground. When a player arrives at Tynecastle, he'll probably sit down and read the paper before the manager comes in and asks if everyone is ready. Now, if that player has been sitting with his knee joints at right angles, and if he's asked for a leg to be fully extended within the next 15 minutes at 20 miles per hour, then the scenario is there for a breakdown. Hearts take a lot of care to try and avoid these situations happening.

"Alex MacDonald even sprung a new one on me when he insisted that players take a bath before they play. This is the beginning of the warm-up where you encourage the circulation to move from the trunk

to the periphery so that the limbs are suffused with blood even before
they have to jog. It is well documented that a bath plus the warm-up can
last up to 60 minutes, so all the substitutes have to do is top up the effort
they put in earlier. Alex and Sandy are both prepared to listen to any
new ideas, and there is no doubt that I have learned a lot from them," he
added.

Rae knows of managers who will override the verdict of the physiotherapist and ask a player to take part in a game when the certainty is
that the individual will break down again. Having said that, he can
recount instances of players reporting injuries that were more mental
than physical in their origin. "When Hearts first came up from the First
to the Premier Division, some of the players struggled to make the
step-up and the injuries they received were as a result of trying to
compete at a higher level than they were capable of attaining. Whatever
team sport you are involved in – and this applies to rugby as well as
football – if players are bursting themselves in a physical sense to
compete, then a higher incidence of injury is bound to arise."

Rae believes that the defensive core of the Hearts side that came out
of the lower league – Henry Smith, Roddy McDonald and Sandy
Jardine – was the early key to the club's success, partly because the trio
were not easily injured and hardly missed a game for the club. When
players do get injured Rae says that knocks fall into two categories –
over-use and direct trauma. The latter is when you get whacked and
there's not much anyone can do about it. The former is when you run
too far or kick too often. "Traumatic injuries will always be with us," he
said. "It is the over-use injuries that are the dangerous ones. Then you
have to recognise when players have done too much and suffer repeated
minor trauma. Fewer games at all grades of football would help and –
who knows? – the quality might also improve."

The physiotherapist credits MacDonald and Jardine with a holistic
approach to the guidance of team matters, helping to blend specialist
knowledge into the jigsaw that makes up the big picture at Tynecastle.
Rae, McNeill and Binnie are part of a back-up team that the
physiotherapist reckons have never had a cross or a hard word in the
past six years. Indeed, there is a persuasive case to be made, which
would find a seconder in the evidence of all three men, that it is out of a
sense of harmony that Hearts' quest for success has been largely
derived.

CHAPTER THIRTEEN

We'll Support You Ever More

MIKE AITKEN

MUCH IS MADE of the strain on players in an age when the fixture list is more crowded than ever before. Perhaps less consideration is given to those loyal supporters who make a point of watching every game their club plays in the course of a season that can seem to last longer than *Gone With The Wind*. In 1987/88, when the Premier Division programme ran to 44 games, it would have cost a supporter of Hearts, even taking subsidised travel into account, almost £1,000 to watch all the club's domestic fixtures. If European travel is added on top of that, it is clear that the pastime of supporting a football club on a regular basis in the 1980s can be a most expensive hobby, quite at odds with the game's cloth-cap image.

While it is probably true to say that the typical football fan remains young, male and working-class, the modern game attracts a broad spectrum of spectators. As this chapter will illustrate, trying to typecast the supporter is a fruitless task. Many more women, youngsters and professional people than is customarily acknowledged enjoy watching the live theatre of football. Indeed, on a Saturday at Tynecastle the centre-stand resembles nothing so much as an outdoor sitting of the Court of Session, with season ticket-holders including a High Court judge, Queen's Counsel, members of the House of Lords, a leading Sheriff and other prominent lawyers.

While the minority of hooligans continue to capture the lion's share of publicity, the real fans in Scotland are no longer lying low. Indeed, supporters are turning out in greater numbers than ever before as the Premier Division continues to buck the European trend of declining gates.

In order to discover some of the reasons for the box-office revival at Tynecastle, I spoke to John Frame, the honorary secretary of the federation of Hearts supporters clubs. Like thousands of others, he joined a supporters club as a 12-year-old, and by the time he'd reached the age of 16 he was a committee member. Having been thrown in at the deep end, he took over as secretary of the federation when he was a student at university. And during the last six years Frame has also run the Junior Club for Hearts. His role, essentially, is to liaise between the supporters – some 45 official clubs with almost 5,000 members – and the football club.

"The majority of clubs are outside Edinburgh and only a handful of the biggest ones have their own premises. What happens, basically, is that people club together for the sake of cheap and convenient transport. There will be the occasional meeting, sometimes weekly, sometimes fortnightly, and many like to organise social events for the members," he said.

"The reasons for joining are not just economic, of course. Many people who own cars and could afford to travel independently join a club because they enjoy being part of a group. The majority of supporters will pay a membership fee as well as the cost of the transport.

"The benefits are that the supporter is guaranteed a ticket for any match, since the tickets for the clubs are put aside before going on sale to the general public. For most big games at Tynecastle, it is true that any supporter will not have a great deal of difficulty getting a ticket. But if you are a member of a club you don't face the inconvenience of having to queue.

"The majority of members prefer to stand on the terracings, but at a recent away game I would estimate that around 12 per cent of the tickets I handled were for the stand. These are people who all want supervised travel and are encouraged to adopt a more responsible attitude," he added.

Hearts supporters have not always enjoyed a good press and Frame acknowledged that there were problems when the club was yo-yoing back and forward between the First and Premier Divisions. "Hearts were going through a lean spell and that had a lot to do with the frustrations of the supporters. It was a bit like peering into a never-ending dark tunnel. But there was also a lot wrong with football in

Scotland at that point – and I think the game has cleaned up its act since then. When Hearts were travelling regularly to places like Dumfries it wasn't the Queen of the South supporters that were coming out to taunt them, but the local yobs who were looking for trouble. It only took one fight to break out and everyone latched on," said Frame.

It is hard enough to believe, for those of us who have found the reporting of certain football matches a bit like entering a war zone where a dispatch is sent back from the front, that it is only a few years since the since the concept of segregation was introduced on the terracings. A history teacher by profession, John Frame says that his pupils find it impossible not to think in terms of a divided support at matches.

As Hearts' results have improved, so has the behaviour of their supporters. In addition, the ground improvements at Tynecastle reflect the desire for a more comfortable environment at matches. Frame makes the point that keeping a stadium in good order is particularly important as a means of denying hooligans the opportunity to cause trouble through exploiting damaged sections of worn terracing. Stones, wood and metal bars can all be dangerous weapons in the wrong hands. "If you take temptation out of people's way, then at least you are not sending an invitation to trouble," he said.

In the battle against the hooligans, Frame reckons that efficient organisation of parking, policing and stewarding of spectators is absolutely essential. He believes that the way in which people are treated outside the ground can also have a bearing on their state of mind inside it. "Six years ago there was an attitude throughout the country that all football supporters were likely to cause trouble and deserved to be treated as potential hooligans. That attitude put people's backs up. Now there has been a mellowing in attitude in Scotland and, as you would expect, the better people are treated the better they behave."

As far as what can be done to improve the supporters' lot in the near future – and the supporters clubs do appreciate that funds are not unlimited – Frame maintains that the quality of the team takes precedence over any other factor. "Having said that, as far as Tynecastle is concerned, the obvious ground improvement concerns the provision of more cover, and I know that plans are afoot on that score. If money is going to be spent on the stadium, then improved toilet facilities are also always going to be in demand.

"Interestingly enough, given the circumstances that prevail at Tynecastle, I don't detect any groundswell of opinion for an all-seated stadium like the one at Pittodrie. People like their comforts, but no one wants to see the capacity cut and it become even more of a scramble to get tickets for matches. Indeed, I would think that Hearts could look at ways to increase the capacity. I understand that an extra 6,000 could be added to the present 29,000 capacity if more exits were installed. Six years ago you could have said put seats in everywhere and no one would have raised a voice in anger, but times have changed," he said.

Hearts have gone out of their way to eliminate the feeling of "them and us" that used to distance the supporters from the club. Part of John Frame's role is to foster a sense of belonging among the fans and make them realise that Tynecastle is no longer the citadel it once was. "I help to organise the mascots at home matches, and while the sponsors can request that facility, at least 50 per cent of the time it is the members of the Junior Supporters club who enjoy that privilege. There are also penalty kick competitions – we had 600 kids at our last open day – tours of the ground, and even an opportunity for some supporters to play on the pitch at Tynecastle, when a competition is staged there. Once there used to be a closed doors policy, but now anyone who wants to see round the place can do so."

Having been secretary of the supporters federation when there were far fewer clubs than there are today, one of the prices of success for John Frame has been the difficulty in meeting the demand for Player of the Year dances. "It was easy when we had ten supporters clubs, but now that there are 45 they have to realise that they can't all get the players they want!" he said.

Hearts draw supporters who travel regularly from Aberdeen, Glasgow, Perth, Kinross, Eyemouth, various parts of Fife and the Borders. There are also groups of fans who travel weekly from London, Manchester, Nottingham and Ireland. Obviously, these individuals will have to be prepared to put out a substantial amount of cash in a season to follow their favoured team. But even for those supporters who watch Hearts and live in the Lothians, the cost of backing their club is not to be sniffed at. "When a club plays 60 games a season, a supporter who pays for a subsidised bus fare, entry to the match and the purchase of a programme, as well as something to eat, is talking about expenditure of not much less than £1,000 a season.

"Given the costs, there is no doubt at all that a much more diverse group of people attend football matches today than in the past. A pupil of mine a couple of years ago undertook a Higher project, examining the economics of the supporters club. We used a couple of clubs as examples and there was no way that we got the findings that were expected. There's a large number of supporters now who come from what used to be described as middle-class or professional backgrounds. I know of one supporters club, for instance, where out of a bus-load of 53, nine or ten of the passengers will be women. There's been a large increase in the number of women attending football in recent years, and of the mail I get from young supporters, a large percentage comes from girls. In our Junior Club at least a fifth of the members are girls. That's a big increase on what you would have found to be the case ten years ago," said Frame.

Hearts reserve a seated section of Tynecastle for parents and children to watch matches together and for members of the Junior Club there is access to the ground and the players that was unheard of in the past. There are also special catering facilities within the family enclosure as well as free gifts from Panini, the company that manufactures football stickers and sponsors the area, as well as discounts on a range of sports goods. Clearly, the aim is to capture the supporters of tomorrow – thus ensuring the continued economic well-being of the club – as well as educating young fans, under supervision, in good habits within the ground. It is also to Hearts' benefit that when a child becomes a member of the Junior Club he has to bring an adult with him. Many who had given up watching football as a bad job have been dragged back to the game kicking and screaming only to find to their amazement that they liked what they saw and in due course have been bitten by the spectating habit again.

Of course there are a number of matches in the fixture list that are less suitable for family viewing than others, and parents who would happily go to the ground with their youngsters on other occasions when the family enclosure was full will not take that risk. "There is no real worry about what might happen inside the ground because the stadium is safe. It is what could happen outside that worries people. Let's face it, the situation at Tynecastle in Gorgie is hardly perfect for the dispersal of supporters," said Frame. "But at the vast majority of games there is no problem at all. And once folk have been persuaded to go and see for themselves that violence is not the problem that it once was, then they've not only been happy to come back themselves but have told others the good news."

Hearts have an excellent relationship with the support today, in part because there is genuine consultation between the club and the fans. "Our views are sought and it is not just a cosmetic exercise," said Frame.

Director Pilmar Smith, who once stood on the terracings himself and enjoyed the company of many of the players in Dave Mackay's time at Tynecastle, is well placed in the boardroom to look out for the interests of the spectators. He has also maintained a connection with the shareholders association, and much of the goodwill that exists between the club and the supporters can be attributed to Smith's efforts. In the past the shareholders used to hold meetings at the University of Edinburgh, but Hearts have opened their doors to the association and kept them informed of developments. Indeed, to this day Pilmar Smith remains on the shareholders committee as well as on the Hearts board.

"Before the present administration at Tynecastle there was no link between the club and the fans – supporters were simply expected to turn up and pay their money at the turnstiles. The fans never got inside Tynecastle and the whole aim seemed to be to keep them at arm's length. In the past, when things were not going so well for the club, the supporters and the shareholders would ask for meetings with the directors – but there was a marked reluctance to discuss any issue.

"Our philosophy is that you should talk to people, and what we do now, both at board and management level, is to respond to letters, whether they be critical of the club, or individuals or whatever, by inviting people to the ground and discussing the matter with them. If you show you are interested in their point of view, then you are more likely to make a friend than an enemy. In short, the problem in the past was that there wasn't enough consultation between the club and its followers, and that is something we've tried hard to put right by providing more direct contact," he said.

A bookmaker by profession, and a friend of Kenny Waugh's for a number of years, Pilmar Smith nonetheless threw his support and that of the shareholders' consortium behind Wallace Mercer – a man he didn't know – when the club was taken over. It was a decision he never regretted. Smith had been a shareholder for a number of years, mainly because of his affection for the club rather than through any ambition to become a director. "I would have loved to be a player, but becoming a director was never a longing that kept me awake at nights," he said. Even so, when Mercer invited Smith on to the board, he was happy to oblige as long as there was a service he could perform for Hearts.

"When I went on to the board I thought that Wallace might want me to help run the lottery or something like that. Instead he told me that there was a job to be done with the supporters, and since I was someone who knew their thoughts, having been amongst them, the responsibility came to me.

"From the start I knew that what the supporters wanted above everything else was a winning team. It is absolutely right that the club gives consideration to improving the facilities, but the number one priority is the team rather than the stadium. There are various things we can do to make Tynecastle a better place for spectators, but some of those projects are in the future. For the moment we've got to help the team to go a stage further and get that right. In the normal course of events, success on the field helps you to generate more money, the extra cash can be used for ground improvements, and everything else falls into place," he said.

An active member of the Labour Party, Pilmar Smith is friendly with Neil Kinnock, the Labour leader. When Smith and Wallace Mercer had lunch with Kinnock, the Leader of the Opposition, who has an interest in football as well as rugby, made the point that certain clubs in England had got themselves into financial hot water by investing enormous sums in new stands at the expense of the team's development. Kinnock's theme was that if you invest money in a player, he can always be sold if the purse-strings need to be tightened. However, it is a little more problematic to move on bricks and mortar.

Smith has led Hearts' campaign against the hooligan element over the years, and while he acknowledges that success can be as big a deterrent as any – "There's usually too much dancing and singing going on for anyone to be concerned with causing bother" – the curbing of the rowdies has only come about because of a lot of hard work and close links with the police.

"We've had a lot of credit, and rightly so, for the way the problem was handled at Tynecastle. The introduction of video cameras, the training of stewards and our work with the police were all steps in the right direction. But you also have to remember that the present board inherited a situation where the previous incumbents had not been paying their police bills. When we took over there was a drawerful waiting for us.

"Our immediate reaction was to try and reduce the cost of policing our home games. I arranged a meeting with the Commander of the West End Division, who had responsibility for our ground. At this time the man in charge was a Chief Superintendent Bert Ridgeway. I would have to give him a lot of credit for the high standards that are maintained at our ground today. He was a first-class policeman, not flexible in any way. His dedication was such that I think his idea of bedtime reading was a perusal of the various Criminal Acts!

"At that first meeting I thought it would be a case of Pilmar and Bert getting together for a cosy chat. Instead, he read the riot act to me. I was given chapter and verse on all the things the club had failed to attend to over the years. Anyway, as far as our request to reduce our police bill was concerned, he told me that we would have to have fewer policemen in our ground – and the only way to achieve that was by improving our stewarding. He said that the responsibility for safety in the ground would always be a police matter, but the introduction of properly trained stewards could have advantages for both the club and the police.

"His view was that his officers would be better employed in the streets catching villains. So Bert Ridgeway offered to help us and show us how to train our stewards. A man called Bill Rodgers was put in charge of the stewarding and we built up a structure of command. The policy of stewarding went from strength to strength and there was the double benefit of improving crowd control – supporters will often act more sensibly if a steward is involved rather than a policeman – and reducing costs," he said.

Indeed, Hearts have been so successful in this respect that in the 1986 edition of the digest of football statistics published by the Football Trust it is revealed that the Edinburgh club have the lowest police costs per 1,000 spectators – £104 in 1986 compared to an average of £182 in the Premier Division, or for that matter in the First Division of the Football League, where the average bill was £170.

Smith was honest enough to acknowledge that expediency played at least as big a part in Hearts' plans to improve crowd control as moral indignation. "The fact of the matter was that we were faced with no option but to get our police costs reduced. Having said that, Bert Ridgeway helped us to set high standards. He was the man who tipped us off about the use of video cameras. Everyone has them now, but we were the first club in Scotland to go to the Football Trust and get a grant to install the cameras at Tynecastle. I struck up a good relationship with Richard Faulkner, now the deputy chairman of the Football Trust but at that time the secretary, and he agreed to give us the money after we'd been to London to present our case. Our operation was so successful that we were used as an example to others of the value of video," he said.

Working on the basis that forewarned is forearmed, over the years Pilmar Smith, secretary Les Porteous and John Frame have liaised with clubs and police forces from Brechin to Paris in a bid to eliminate problems regarding supporters. "But we take an interest in the well-being of our fans, and if you give them a sense of responsibility, then they will react to that in the right way," he said.

While Tynecastle has become known as the good ideas factory of Scottish football, few people know that the original suggestion for the appointment of a retired police officer as a security adviser to the SFA came from Hearts. The matter arose in a discussion between Pilmar Smith and Wallace Mercer which the chairman then mooted in the corridors of power. Today, not only the SFA but also Rangers and Celtic employ operations officers.

No one would dispute that Hearts have taken meaningful strides behind the scenes to reduce hooliganism. However, there have still been instances of adverse publicity in recent years – the throwing of bananas at the Rangers winger Mark Walters, for instance, caused a great hoo-ha in the media – and Pilmar Smith appreciates that you rest on your laurels at your peril. "You mustn't become complacent and think things are easy. Sometimes you have to give yourself a shake, because if you think the problem is solved, that's when your troubles can really begin," he said.

In spite of all the publicity they attract, it is a fact that the troublemakers are in a small minority. Dealing with the club's supporters involves a much wider brief than just handling the hooligans. I asked Pilmar Smith how he saw the way ahead in improving the decent supporter's lot.

"Our family enclosure has worked as well as we could have hoped, and is evidence that you have to do more than just talk about the need to attract a family audience to football – you have to give them the facilities that will bring them back. Apart from parents and children, we also realise that there are more women going to football than ever before. It used to be the case that women didn't choose to stand on the terracing; but that has changed, and at the start of last season we appreciated early on that we would have to increase the ladies' toilet facilities. Our Junior Club has been a great success, and you can't ignore the fact that the more interest you create amongst youngsters, the more adults are likely to come with them," he said.

If the man who pays cash at the turnstile is the original sponsor of a football match, clubs have had to adjust and improve their facilities accordingly to attract the backing of the business community. "Our business and executive clubs have helped to attract support from companies who can afford to spend that bit more on enjoying the best we have to offer. There's no doubt from the club's point of view that their money is a necessary source of income. At the end of the day our aim must be to look after all of our supporters to the best of our ability," said Smith.

As far as the Marshall Food Group at Newbridge in Midlothian are concerned – Marshall's Chunky Chicken are one of the leading local firms who sponsor matches at Tynecastle – Hearts have delivered on all the promises that enticed the fastest-growing company in Scotland to spend part of their promotional budget with a football club. Colin Wilson is the sales and marketing director with Marshall's, and he has no doubt about the fact that his company decided to get involved with Hearts for purely commercial reasons. "Anything we do must have a commercial spin-off. Our arrangement with Hearts meant exposure of our name. When we struck up the arrangement with Hearts three years ago we took advertising space in the programme, boards in advantageous position were placed in the stadium and a certain amount of entertaining facilities were made available to us and our customers," he said.

Marshall's felt they were taking something of a gamble when they got on board with Hearts in 1985, for the Edinburgh club were not the force then that they are now, with a buoyant support and extensive media coverage. "For us, it was a gamble that paid off," Wilson added. "From the day we became involved as a sponsor Hearts became increasingly successful, and their unbeaten run of 31 games in the 1985/86 season was tremendous public relations for us. We were able to say in the trade papers – 'Look, we're feeding these lads chicken and no one can beat this team'. It worked so well that every time a butcher from England would come on the 'phone with an order they'd say, 'Oh, I see they won again'. It was a marvellous sales promotion exercise, and it was a situation where we happened to get lucky.

"But the big thing from our point of view, of course, in terms of exposure, is the television coverage. There are other clubs we could have been involved with who would not have attracted anything like the attention Hearts have received. We've taped on video certain matches at Tynecastle and the exposure we get on television in Scotland occasionally on the network programmes is worth an awful lot of money if you are having to buy the time. Not only that, but exposure in the context of football is public relations rather than advertising. We've got involved with Hearts' Junior Club and produced a poster for them. When we did that, it was clearly to our benefit that our name was going on the walls of 5,000 kids' bedrooms, and maybe catching the eye of the lady of the house."

Marshall's appreciate that in order to make a sponsorship work – even if it is on a modest scale compared to shirt advertising – the company has to develop promotional ideas. In addition, there needs to be the right kind of co-operation from the club: action in support of promises. "Hearts have been exceptionally co-operative, and their players have worked well with us. So much so that we've become disproportionately associated with them. People all over Britain, and in Scotland particularly, say to us, 'You're the people who are involved with Hearts'. This kind of reaction is quite beyond the kind of money we put in. We've maximised our association and made it work well for us," he said.

Marshall's are more than pleased, then, with the amount of exposure they've earned from their involvement with a football club. The image Hearts project is very much to their liking. "If there were riots at Hearts matches and hooligans were involved in fights every week, we just couldn't be involved with them," said Wilson. "We can only be involved with a responsible club that has a responsible attitude to these matters. The image of the club must be complementary to our product. And, of course, the more successful Hearts are, the more exposure there is for those of us who sponsor them. Our involvement with Hearts is a sound commercial proposition. We're not in the charity business as far as football is concerned. We made a careful appraisal of what we were getting – and our advertising boards are seen by millions."

As far as the facilities for entertaining the sponsor's customers are concerned, Colin Wilson described the Tynecastle set-up as excellent. Valued business clients who spend a great deal of money with Marshall's are given an afternoon out that is more personalised and specialised than other forms of entertaining.

Marshall's have had numerous approaches from other clubs to sponsor matches, but the company take the view that you can spread the butter too thinly. In return for their cash, a match sponsor requires good facilities, a trouble-free image on the terracings, and a team successful enough to project the right kind of exposure for the company.

On a much grander scale, Scottish Brewers, the largest backers of sport in Scotland with an outlay considerably in excess of £1 million a year, have found a similar pattern for success at Ibrox. The McEwan's Lager sponsorship of Rangers is the most lucrative deal in Scottish football. Apart from providing extra funds which played a part in backing the Ibrox revolution, Scottish Brewers also did themselves a favour by identifying a young brand of lager with a famous football team. The impact on the market-place was dramatic, with cans of lager in particular gaining substantial sales at a time when demand in general was declining.

The deal with Rangers lasts until the summer of 1990. "We look upon our partnership with Rangers as a marriage rather than a brief affair," said managing director Tony Belfield. "When we sponsored Rangers that wasn't the end of our involvement but the beginning; what we have with Rangers isn't patronage but an active business venture."

While the deal with Rangers is the single biggest aspect of Scottish Brewers' involvement with the football scene, it is by no means the only one. The Younger's Tartan Special Player and Manager of the Month awards have been a regular part of the scene for a number of years, having previously been known as Mackinlay's personality awards.

Dundee, Hibs and Hearts all get backing for individual matches, while the Tynecastle club also benefited last season from a Scottish Brewers loan which helped the club to improve off-the-field facilities. At a grass-roots level, Scottish Brewers give some backing to the Scottish Welfare Cup, the North of Scotland Football League, and to various testimonials. Last season the testimonial game for Jim Duffy of Dundee and Tommy Burns's highly successful match between Celtic and Liverpool were supported by the company, as was Celtic's dinner to commemorate their centenary.

In the late 1970s Younger's Tartan sponsored the Scottish Cup. Belfield bided his time on that venture until the SFA were willing to show the final live on television, and Scottish Brewers can take some credit for improving the packaging of the final. Although it was generally thought that hooliganism – and the link between alcohol abuse and trouble on the terracings – was the sole reason for Scottish Brewers pulling out of the sponsorship, Tony Belfield also regarded the cost of renewal as too high.

If the product is right, however, as it was at Ibrox, Scottish Brewers were not to be deterred by a high asking price. "The amount of money we've put into Rangers has been described as obscene. But for us it has been a cost-effective exercise. The budget is the equivalent of a small television campaign and provides us with a good business partnership. We bring something to Rangers and they deliver other things to us," said Belfield.

Outwith football, the rugby scene benefits from sponsorship of the McEwan's National League and Inter-District championship, while minority sports like yachting and amateur snooker also get a helping hand. Scottish Brewers pride themselves on knowing how to make the best of sponsoring sport – both for themselves and for the sports concerned. "The object isn't only just to sell more beer," commented the managing director. "Of course we're happy when that happens. But there are also things that we do which could either turn out to be good advertising for the company or may be for the good of the community. Our involvement with Rangers has attracted such massive attention that it is easy to overlook the fact that we do provide support for no fewer than 28 football club in Scotland and we strive to help the game in general."

CHAPTER FOURTEEN

Spirited Progress

MIKE AITKEN

THERE HAS BEEN more talk about money in Scottish football over the past couple of years than just about any other topic you care to mention. The massive investment made by Rangers in new players, Celtic's positive response in the transfer market, and Aberdeen's willingness to recruit international footballers from the Football League have all added glamour to the Premier Division.

In the opinion of Alex MacDonald, however, cash is not the only factor in the construction of a quality football team. Certainly, it can make life easier as a manager when your only concern is having to buy the best. But those who don't enjoy access to more or less unlimited funds learn quickly to compensate in other areas.

"Every time we played Rangers last season it seemed that they'd bought a new player," MacDonald recalled. "Celtic also spent big, and in future the Old Firm will invest again. So it is going to get more difficult to win things, not easier.

"As a club, Hearts do have a substantial amount of money to spend compared to the likes of Dundee and Motherwell. But we are trying to compete in a different market, the one along with Rangers and Celtic where you want to win things. I don't think most people appreciate just how difficult that is.

"If there is a theme that runs through Hearts, then it is the spirit of the club. What comes through all the time is the backbone of the players. The qualities of grit and enthusiasm are among our biggest

154

No Hearts player in 1988 impressed more than Dave McPherson, the club's £350,000 signing from Rangers.

assets. The spirit has been there since the start, and we've not lost it along the way even though the players have changed and the quality has improved. It is something you can't buy. Nor does it just come together as if by magic – we've worked at it and nursed it over the years. The way the club is today happened more by design than accident," he said.

The management team of MacDonald and Sandy Jardine regarded the 1987/88 season as another year of progress for Hearts even if a major honour continued to elude them. Jardine reckoned that Hearts played their best football since his arrival at Tynecastle from Rangers in 1982. "I accept we didn't win something, and everyone here is geared up for success. But it was a year when we made definite strides forward and put our most polished product ever on the park. Some of our displays reached a very high standard indeed. I would go as far as to say that if we'd played as well in the year when we were pipped by Celtic for the title on the last day, then we would have won the Championship easily," he said.

No Hearts player in 1988 impressed MacDonald and Jardine more than Dave McPherson, the club's £350,000 signing from Rangers. The centre-half was asked to change his style and attack the ball more at Tynecastle than he had done at Ibrox. Initially McPherson made one or two slips, and there were some who doubted the wisdom of investing so much cash in the young defender. In fact, both in partnership with Craig Levein and Brian Whittaker, McPherson went from strength to strength as the year unfolded, and was on the fringes of the international team. "I needed a while to settle in, but getting the opportunity to play regularly in one position rather than chopping and changing all the time helped me no end," said the big centre-half.

Henry Smith, a couple of gaffes at Hampden against Celtic in a Scottish Cup semi-final notwithstanding, John Colquhoun and Gary Mackay also enjoyed an excellent season, winning their first caps and making Hearts one of the most consistent sides in the course of a demanding 44-game championship. In order to give a flavour of the football year, Hearts co-manager Sandy Jardine here gives a month-by-month analysis of his team's fortunes, charting their progress from the preparatory work of a summer tour in July to the heartbreaking climax of an agonising defeat from Celtic at Hampden in April.

JULY: We'd bought a couple of new faces in Hugh Burns and Dave McPherson and were looking forward to welcoming back Craig Levein in the not-too-distant future. I was planning to retire once Dave and Craig teamed up together, and the future looked bright when we set off for our five-game tour of West Germany.

We played fixtures against Homburg, Preussen Munster, Bad Kreuznach, Birkenfeld and Remscheid. Although we lost a couple of games, the object of the exercise was to get everyone fit and give the new lads a chance to fit in. It was a first-class pre-season exercise in which we were able to try things and experiment away from critical eyes. When we came home we were optimistic about the year that lay in front of us, and though we hadn't set any specific targets we were hopeful of moving up from fifth place in the League to finishing somewhere in the top four.

Henry Smith was one of the club's best ever signings and it was an important day when he agreed to sign a new three-year contract.

AUGUST: Our first match of the 1987/88 season was against Falkirk at Tynecastle. We played with a lot of skill and purpose that day, though our concentration wavered near the end and some of the edge was taken off a handsome performance. But we played a lot of good football from the back in a 4-2 victory. Understandably, Dave McPherson needed time to find his feet and had a shaky game. Yet we were pleased with the quality of our overall form and travelled to Celtic Park in confident mood.

Against Celtic we produced a disciplined effort that merited a draw. However, a number of refereeing decisions went against us and we lost a

controversial goal three minutes from time when Mark McGhee fouled
Dave McPherson before putting the ball in the net. Somehow it was to
be the story of our season, losing goals in the dying minutes against
Celtic. We came away from Glasgow feeling disappointed at getting
nothing, but still positive about our general prospects.

The rest of the month was notable for a sparkling performance
against Kilmarnock in the Skol Cup when we blitzed them with six
goals. That set us up for the visit of Dundee United and what was to be
one of our happiest afternoons of the season.

The quality of our football had been getting better and better. That
day everything came together for us. We played some magnificent
football and destroyed the Tannadice club, with their wealth of
international defenders, 4-1. Sandy Clark, John Robertson and Ian
Jardine got the goals, but the key to our success was the way the team
gelled as a unit. The boost everyone got from the United result carried
over into our remaining fixtures that month with comfortable victories
over Hibs and Clyde in the Skol Cup.

SEPTEMBER: The 2-0 win over Clyde sent us into a fourth-round
Skol Cup tie against Rangers at Ibrox. The players wanted to do well at
Ibrox and all the signs were that we would push Graeme Souness's men
close. But on the night Rangers played to a good standard and we struck
rock bottom. As far as we were concerned it was a recipe for disaster,
and there was no question that Rangers thoroughly merited their 4-1
win. Some of our players suffered from stage-fright that night. A lot
had been expected of us after playing so well in earlier games, but we let
ourselves down. At least we learned a few lessons that stood us in good
stead for future trips to Ibrox.

Having begun so miserably, September could have been a soul-
destroying month for us. Instead the players, to their credit, bounced
back and reeled off a sequence of four straight League wins over
Morton, Motherwell, Dundee and Dunfermline. Without being
brilliant, we kept churning out the results and had settled into a
consistent groove.

OCTOBER: Like the previous month, our programme began with a
game against Rangers. They were just back from a European mission
abroad and seemed happy enough to come to Tynecastle for a point. It
was a dour, uncompromising type of game. Over the 90 minutes we
were the better side but couldn't break the goalless deadlock. More
important than the result was the fact that Craig Levein made a

successful comeback to competitive first-team action after being missing for almost a year. I stepped down that day and effectively retired after 25 years as a player. Our win over Aberdeen, after falling behind to an early penalty, was notable for one of the goals of the season from Dave McPherson, an absolutely superb strike that will go down as one of the best shots seen at Tynecastle in years. We went on from there to travel to Brockville. The team was scoring goals quite freely at that stage and our 5-1 win over Falkirk was a stunning performance on a most awkward pitch.

The one setback for the club this month was the 2-1 defeat by our old rivals Hibs. On the day we didn't think the scoreline reflected the run of play, but overall we had no complaints for luck had been mostly on our side for years in the Edinburgh derby. Though we would have happily kept up our winning sequence against Hibs, the one bonus of the defeat was that it deflated the pressure that was growing on the players. We tried to defuse the situation when we talked about the match to the media, but it was inevitable that we would get beaten sooner or later. And, of course, Hibs had started to put their house in order, signing new players and providing a sterner test for us than they had done in previous seasons. I'd be very surprised if either side dominates this derby match in the near future the way we had done for so long.

Our knack of shrugging off disappointment helped us to get back on the rails with convincing three-goal wins over Morton and Motherwell. And before the month was out there was another special performance to savour. Our 4-2 win over Dundee was one of the highlights of the season. We were 3-0 up at half-time when the pace and the quality of our football had left Dundee shellshocked. Quite frankly it could have been six or seven, but we took our foot off the accelerator in the second half and Dundee got a couple of consolation goals.

NOVEMBER: There was another full house at Tynecastle for the visit of Celtic, who played splendidly in an open and entertaining first half. If Billy McNeill's players had the edge before the interval, we were the better team in the second half. John Colquhoun scored a spectacular goal that was frequently replayed in television highlights of the season's best. Celtic were reduced to ten men when Mick McCarthy was rather harshly shown the red card and got a late goal against the run of play through Mark McGhee after good work by Roy Aitken. It left us feeling that the rub of the green in a match against Celtic had gone against us yet again – but there was no cause for despondency since we'd maintained our unbeaten home record against an excellent side.

We balanced the books after dropping a point against Celtic by going to Pittodrie and earning a valuable draw. Those displays set us up nicely for a midweek visit to Tannadice, where the television cameras captured yet another first-class effort against Dundee United. We secured a 3-0 victory and fully exploited the problems that United had been facing with injuries. The scoreline didn't really tell you just how superior we were that evening. Oddly, we followed up that high with a relative low against St Mirren when we had 99.99 per cent of the play but somehow couldn't score a goal. At one stage we forced eight consecutive corners and still couldn't put the ball in the back of the net!

We tended to do to Dunfermline in the year what Celtic did to us, and our 3-2 win over the Fifers was notable for a late fight-back in which the last-gasp goals earned us both points. That match was notable for the first appearance of Mike Galloway, our £60,000 signing from Halifax. He did well that night and convinced Alex and me that he was worth a run from the start.

Our next match was at Ibrox, and even though we lost again 3-2, the team's performance was much improved on our dismal effort in the Skol Cup. Mike did extremely well and capped a fine individual debut with a terrific goal. He was to be a fixture in the team from then on and proved himself to be an outstanding acquisition.

We'd changed our team in view of what we'd learned from our last trip to Ibrox, and I honestly believe we played them off the park that day. What went wrong was that we made three blunders in defence and were severely punished each time. It was a sickener for everyone, having played so well, to get nothing for our efforts. But everyone was determined that before the season was out we would have a point to make at Ibrox.

DECEMBER: After a deserved win over a very defensive Falkirk side, it was time to cross swords with Celtic again at Parkhead. This turned out to be another one of our 'nearly' days when the players did ever so well but didn't get the reward their efforts merited. We were leading 2-0 through goals from Robertson and Galloway and looked to have the points sealed until a late penalty brought Celtic back into the match. You have to be careful what you say about these things, but let's just say that if an infringement did take place, most neutrals felt the incident was outside the penalty box.

The penalty goal, not surprisingly, gave Celtic a massive lift. It brought them right back into things, and Paul McStay went on to score a late equaliser with a well-struck shot. To make matters worse, we all

When Craig Levein was again stricken by injury Brian Whittaker moved to centre-half to enjoy one of his best-ever seasons.

felt that we had a far stronger penalty claim than Celtic's turned down. All credit to Celtic, who came back from a position where they looked dead and buried; but having been by far the better team, we look back on that game with a sense of injustice.

I think the disappointment of the last few minutes at Parkhead took something out of us, and we moved into a spell where the goals dried up. A draw at home to Motherwell was followed by goalless matches at Dens Park and Cappielow. If we wanted to look for reasons as to why the title slipped away from us, then those draws clearly did us no favours. It goes without saying that the old year went out on a low note in Greenock when we made and missed a hatful of chances.

JANUARY: The new year began, frustratingly, with another blank. Against Hibs in the Ne'erday fixture, it took a quite breathtaking performance from Andy Goram to keep us at bay. The Hibs goalkeeper had a memorable match, pulling off a series of unbelievable saves in the first half.

Thankfully, the goalscoring drought came to an end at East End Park. We scored four times, and the mood amongst the players had received the ideal fillip before our next encounter with Rangers.

One of the most encouraging aspects of the season for us was the manner in which Craig Levein and Dave McPherson were developing their partnership in central defence. The two players were improving all the time, and we had high hopes for the pair of them. But after making his comeback against Rangers in October, it was most unfortunate that Craig should hurt his knee again in the same fixture. He was to play no further part in our season, and the development was a bad blow to the club. By comparison, the game itself paled into insignificance, though once more we held the upper hand without turning pressure into a winning advantage.

We had to reorganise the defence for our next match against Dundee United. Both Neil Berry and Mike Galloway could have played at the back, but their drive was valuable in midfield. Brian Whittaker had experience of the centre-half position in his days with Partick Thistle and we thought he could do well there. In fact, Whittaker and McPherson were to surpass all expectations and the partnership they struck up was a real bonus for us.

After a more typical encounter with Dundee United – they were over a spate of injuries and back to their best at closing down the opposition – we travelled to Brockville in the Scottish Cup and were hit by another injury blow. This time it was the club captain, Walter Kidd, who was about to go into cold storage and would not kick another ball before the season ended. The knee injury sustained by our experienced right-back was another difficulty in that it cut down our options in defence. After losing two captains in the space of a fortnight it was just as well that Dave McPherson accepted even more responsibility at the back. He went from strength to strength over the next four months and was our most consistent player.

As far as the Cup tie at Falkirk was concerned, we expected that to be a difficult draw because of the tight park and the competitive approach of the opposition. The conditions underfoot were nothing short of terrible and we had to adjust our style and play a different type of football. It wasn't an afternoon for silky soccer. We fell behind in the first half but equalised almost immediately and went on to run out convincing winners. The fixture was as awkward as we'd suspected it might be, but we came through the test with flying colours.

FEBRUARY: The month began with one of those days that crop up all too infrequently in the course of a season, when everything you hit in front of goal seems to end up in the back of the net. We defeated St Mirren 6-0 at Paisley, though we actually had less of the play than in the 0-0 game at Tynecastle.

We followed that up with a drawn match against Aberdeen best remembered for a highly controversial penalty decision that denied us both points. A speculative high ball struck Ian Jardine's shoulder in the last minute of the game, and after the referee had awarded a penalty Aberdeen grabbed a point that had looked beyond them.

The fourth round of the Scottish Cup brought us a home tie against Morton at Tynecastle which was a strangely low-key affair. Whether the familiarity of meeting a team from the lower end of the Premier Division had bred a little contempt amongst the players I couldn't say, but we went about our job in a professional manner and won the tie with plenty in hand.

Around this time the speculation began in the Press about John Robertson's future. Whether or not this had an effect on the team is open to debate, but if we wanted to go back and find a day when the Championship edged away from us, it was at Brockville on 27 February.

Oddly enough, in the first half of that game against Falkirk we played with a bit of style. The quality of our outfield play on a tricky surface was excellent, but we contrived to miss half-a-dozen chances. In the Premier Division that kind of generosity will always backfire on you.

True enough, Falkirk stuck away the first real opening they'd made in the game and clinched the points with a late goal that meant there was no way back for us. There's no doubt in my mind that defeat was the result which knocked us back from Celtic.

MARCH: One of the features of the present Hearts squad is their resilience, and we got back on the rails at Fir Park with a win over Motherwell. Tommy McLean's men had more of the play at the start, but we ran out of good winners and the win set us up for an important Cup tie against Dunfermline.

The game had the atmosphere of a local derby, and after the excitement generated by Dunfermline's win over Rangers in the previous round, everyone expected a close and a thrilling match. Football, however, has an endless capacity for turning up tales of the unexpected. This one was a tie we won 3-0, but truthfully it could have been a lot more. It was a victory achieved with surprising ease against a Dunfermline side that, for some mysterious reason, didn't play on the day.

The rest of the month was made up of some bread-and-butter performances – a win over a weakened Dundee side, a draw with Hibs in a poor derby, and a win at Morton. Although the pursuit of Celtic in the title race was by now a lost cause, we remained determined to finish in as high a League position as we possibly could.

APRIL: It wasn't only the will to chase second place, but also the desire to show we could win at Ibrox, that motivated the players in the 2-1 victory over Rangers. Psychologically it meant a lot to us, and it would do the team no harm in the future to remember how they'd gone to Glasgow and beaten Rangers for the first time since Graeme Souness took over. I thought we deserved our win in front of a 40,000 crowd. And the more you beat the Old Firm the more you start to build up a bank of confidence for future meetings. That result was undoubtedly significant for us.

From Ibrox we went on the following week to Hampden and our biggest game of the season. A 65,000 crowd turned out to watch the Scottish Cup semi-final against Celtic. The game had the atmosphere associated with the final itself. Although hopes of a quality encounter had been high, it turned out to be an ordinary match because the performances of the two forward lines both fell way below standard. We took the lead through a goal that looked controversial when Dave McPherson challenged Pat Bonner and Brian Whittaker's lob sailed into the net.

John Robertson was the favourite son before he moved to Newcastle United – but he'll always be welcome back at Tynecastle.

Having got our noses in front thanks to a mistake on Bonner's part, Celtic put us under a tremendous amount of pressure. But a combination of solid defending and slack finishing helped us to keep them at bay. By the time we got to the closing minutes, Celtic were reduced to hitting high balls and looked like a side that had run out of ideas.

Then a couple of errors on the part of our goalkeeper, Henry Smith, gifted Celtic two goals in the last three minutes of the tie. I've had many highs and lows as a player and manager during 25 years in football, but I'd never experienced the sense of disappointment that hit me that day. I was absolutely gutted. It would have been bad enough to have drawn the game. But then to suffer another self-inflicted wound and lose a place in the final through our own fault was mighty hard to take. If anything, the feeling was even more acute than the day the Championship slipped from our grasp at Dens Park. I suppose, to look on the bright side, at least we're getting closer to success. We've cut the losing margin from 17 minutes to 17 seconds – maybe next time we'll go all the way!

Once again, however, the players showed their character by refusing to feel sorry for themselves. It was impossible for Alex and me to lift the side in our next game against Dunfermline. The players had to lift themselves, and we made a number of changes in a bid to freshen things.

We didn't play all that well, and fell a goal behind early in the match. To come back as we did and score twice in the last four minutes to secure a win must go down as one of our gutsiest-ever performances. Everyone, including the managers, had been in a daze before the match. But the players kept plugging away for 90 minutes and we felt proud of the way they earned that result. The victory kept us in second place and delayed Celtic's Championship celebration.

When Billy McNeill brought his players to Tynecastle on the Saturday we remained just as keen to delay the party for another week. We also felt it would be a feather in our cap to become the first side to defeat Celtic since the autumn.

Billy McNeill's side began well but missed a lot of chances. After Mike Galloway took advantage of a slip by Pat Bonner we gained control, and in a spirited second-half performance we were the better side as Gary Mackay scored a second goal. Mark McGhee, who had a knack of scoring against us, got one back for Celtic, but we managed to avoid shooting ourselves in the foot this time.

The win took us further ahead of Rangers, though it was another setback to lose Gary Mackay, our captain, with a fractured cheek for the remainder of the season.

We followed up the encouraging win over Celtic with another excellent result away to Aberdeen. Our lads created the better chances in a goalless draw at Pittodrie and we ended the season unbeaten against the Dons.

I'm afraid we seemed to go off the boil after those performances, and our final home match against St Mirren produced an unacceptable display. We lost a bad goal in a sloppy performance, and thereby surrendered our unbeaten home record as well as missing out on the chance to clinch second place in the Championship. Even if we'd managed a draw – which should not have been beyond the players, although we were short on the day – the team could have gone to the supporters and taken a bow for their efforts. It had been almost a year since we 'd lost at Tynecastle, and there were no excuses for bowing out on such a low note.

MAY: Ironically, Hibs did us a turn by going to Pittodrie and beating Aberdeen 2-0, a result that assured us of second place in the Premier Division regardless of the outcome of our final match against Dundee United at Tannadice. Even though we were missing a lot of first-team players, the lads buckled down at Tannadice and maintained their unbeaten record for the season against the Scottish Cup finalists. Dave McPherson was quite superb in that last game and marshalled a young team to a creditable draw. His form was such that it was hard to understand how he wasn't figuring in the international reckoning.

After the season was over, all that was left was for the players to enjoy a short break on Spain's Costa del Sol before enjoying a well-earned rest during the close season. For Alex and me, though, there was the small matter of strengthening the first-team squad and making sure Hearts came back in the 1988/89 season better equipped for an assault on the honours than ever before.

The football year would come full circle for us with another trip to West Germany and a chance to introduce Eamonn Bannon and Iain Ferguson to the rest of the team.

CHAPTER FIFTEEN

Through the Looking-Glass

WALLACE MERCER

THE IMAGE of the game of football and the impression projected by Hearts are important issues for me. We live in an age of communication and football ignores the media – and how radio, television and the rest present the sport to their audience – at its peril.

I became actively involved on the inside of the game in Scotland in 1981. However, a watershed year had taken place the previous season when the Scottish Cup final at Hampden was marred by rioting and the game's status in Scotland was badly tarnished. If that black day had a bright underside, it was the eventual introduction of the Criminal Justice Act, which, amongst other things, put a stop to alcohol being taken into grounds. Here at last was a sign that the judiciary and the politicians were willing to get behind football's legislators in a bid to clean up the game's act.

There's no doubt that thanks to matters coming to a head at that juncture, the disease of hooliganism which had begun to spread through the Scottish scene was diagnosed, treated and subsequently prevented from developing into the cancer that was to blight the game in England. A nadir was surely reached in Brussels in 1985 when the European Cup final between Juventus and Liverpool was prefaced by unprecedented scenes of mayhem on the terraces of the Heysel Stadium. On top of the tragic loss of life at Bradford, the deaths in Brussels all but brought English football to its knees.

In Scotland, perhaps it was a case of "there but for fortune", but the memory of mounted policemen charging across Hampden on horseback in a bid to quell the disturbances after the Rangers v Celtic Cup final of 1979/80 was a chilling one and precipitated meaningful action from all those with football's best interests at heart. For what kind of state of affairs was it to be associated with violence of such numbing mindlessness? I recall being at Wembley that day to watch an FA Cup final between Arsenal and Manchester United and viewing the scenes on television from the sanctuary of a sponsors' lounge. It was nothing short of tumultuous, and it was interesting at the time to note the casual reaction from English colleagues who felt that similar developments south of the border were impossible.

When I became the majority shareholder at Tynecastle seven years ago, I was aware that Hearts also had a problem associated with hooligan behaviour. It was a complex matter, wrapped up with lack of success, a dwindling support and an element of religious bigotry. My own belief was that the decline on the field of play had done much to create the atmosphere for the lowering of standards on the terracings. And, on top of that, the lack of leadership emanating from the boardroom meant that the club was not perceived as taking a stand against such antisocial behaviour. Hence there was an absence of community spirit and the club and the community were in danger of becoming alienated from one another.

Our problem at Tynecastle was hardly unique in Scotland at that period, but that didn't mean we could sit back and let events take their course. There was back-up in the form of the aforementioned Criminal Justice Act and the SFA entered the fray with a campaign to contain serious foul play on the field. But we also had to take a stand. From 1981 to 1983 we initiated moves to introduce video cameras and increase stewarding at Tynecastle. There was also an attempt in other areas to help supporters feel that they belonged, and a sense of responsibility was required on their part to put the activities of the minority of troublemakers into perspective. I'm not for one second trying to suggest that we solved our problems overnight. But as important as anything else was the bond of trust that was built up between the fans and the club. We were not going to sell them down the river. Better times were coming.

That faith was justified not only in the turnaround at Tynecastle but also in the collective success story of Scottish football over the past five years. The massive investment made by Rangers has attracted more publicity than any other recent development, and while that was a major shot in the arm, it is worth bearing in mind that gates were already dramatically on the increase before the revolution at Ibrox.

My personal view about the impact of Rangers' success on the economics of the Scottish game is that it has not enticed any new people into our grounds, but there has been a redefinition of where people choose to watch the game. Standards have improved on and off the field, and for the last five years all the top clubs in Scotland have made strides.

You can massage statistics to back up just about any point of view you like, but I do think it was a most significant point that no fewer than 53 per cent of the paying public north of the border only attended four stadia last year – namely Ibrox, Parkhead, Tynecastle and Pittodrie. In short, the gulf between those at the top and the rest is on the increase. A club like Meadowbank Thistle, who have done well coming out of the Second Division into a competitive place in the First, will only attract in the course of a season what a club like Hearts will draw in one gate.

I'll deal with this particular subject at greater length in a subsequent chapter, but what has happened in both Scotland and England is a concentration of business strength which has led to the creation of an economic élite in the Football League as well as in the Premier Division.

Getting back to the topic in question, that is to define the image of football and how the sport is viewed by the general public, I believe that there's been an enormous change for the better since I first became directly involved seven years ago. As far as my own club is concerned, I believe that Hearts have two fundamentally important assets – the players and the supporters.

Apart from being the first club in Scotland to introduce the video cameras and our own stewarding system, we also looked at the relationship between Hearts and the people who paid their money at the gate. We felt that relationship could and should be improved, and that's why we went to the trouble of appointing a director whose role it was to liaise between Hearts and the supporters. I've tried to build a relationship with the supporters over the years, but I knew full well that I could not present myself as a punters' man. Living as I do, I couldn't pretend to a working-class dimension. That's where Pilmar Smith came into the picture, and his role has been a significant one at Tynecastle over the years. His job was to keep in touch with the views and feelings of the bulk of the club's customers.

When I took over as chairman in the early 1980s I was a youngish man in my mid-thirties who had been chairman of Edinburgh Round Table, on the lookout to become involved in a community project. As things

Another "Full House" looks on as Dave McPherson beats Terry Butcher to the ball.

worked out, I couldn't have taken part in a venture with more community links than the running of a football club. My philosophy and approach to getting involved with Hearts was thus: it's got no money but a marvellous tradition and the scope for almost endless improvement. It didn't require a football expert or a business genius to work out that the two key elements needed to make Hearts successful again were players and supporters.

I was prepared to do just about anything to raise capital in the first couple of years, but we never lost sight of the value of our place in the community. I remember attending a board meeting at a time when things were not going all that well for the club and there were a lot of long faces sitting round the boardroom table. We were under great pressure because of an unpaid police bill, as I recall, and a mood of glum consternation hung over the proceedings.

On the car radio I'd heard driving to this meeting that unemployment had gone through the three million barrier for the first time in memory.

I told my fellow directors that given the problems the rest of the country was facing, our difficulties were trivial. We had a home game against Motherwell on the Saturday and I suggested to my colleagues that instead of sitting there feeling sorry for ourselves we should let the unemployed in for nothing. Anyone who could present a UB40 was allowed entry without charge. It was a gesture on our part in recognition of the world outwith football, though unfortunately the match itself wasn't up to much and turned out to be a pretty dull affair. One newspaper in fact did a light piece saying it was just as well that Hearts had let half the crowd in for nothing, for the other half were surely robbed! We repeated the exercise a few times after that, but on reflection decided that to implement a free gate on a permanent basis would be doing a disservice to others and could have led to an abuse of the system. At any rate, even before Pilmar Smith came on board, we were trying to establish social links and build a rapport with the supporters.

As to my own relationship with the fans, I think they respect me because I've kept my promises. We were not prepared to sell off the club's main asset – the outstanding young players on the books – for short-term gain. That helped us to stabilise the club, and from there we've gone on to build up the business to the point where almost 30 per cent of our customers come to our home matches in family groups.

There's been an evolution, both at Hearts and in Scottish football in general, over the past few years, with a far greater willingness on the part of Rangers, Celtic and Aberdeen to spend to keep themselves at the forefront of the game. The new wealth in football emanates from sponsorship, from businessmen who are putting cash into the sport because they believe it is a commercial enterprise under control.

Football has put its house in order in Scotland, but that doesn't mean to say there is now time for resting on laurels or indulging in self-congratulation. As far as the question of hooliganism is concerned, one is constantly trying to keep the tin lid on the problem. I don't think there will ever be an absolute solution to that kind of rowdy behaviour.

As to the standards on the field of play, the SFA have tried to eliminate violent conduct, but whether or not they've dealt adequately with certain incidents that have taken place in the last year or two is perhaps open to question. I'm not convinced that the association has always come down hard enough on certain patterns of behaviour involving groups of players being ordered off.

Particularly at a time when business is taking such an active interest in football, the kind of publicity that attends field misbehaviour does nothing for the image or the status of the game. I appreciate that football is a man's game, but if the laws are not adhered to then the simple fact of the matter is that we won't have a sport of any consequence at all in future.

I do a fair amount of after-dinner speaking in Scotland, and when people come up to talk to me they say that they know I run Hearts with a strong hand and the club will not be permitted to get out of control. I believe implicitly in the value of speaking directly to the supporters. Last season, when John Robertson had come in asking for a £100,000 signing-on fee and £1,000 a week in wages, the first people to know were the supporters. After a board meeting at Tynecastle I went on television and made it quite clear that this was a situation we were not prepared to tolerate any longer. I had to make it known that we had other players to keep happy and the prodigal son was not going to be treated any differently from the rest.

I'm not the type who surrounds himself with public relations experts, and sometimes when I appear on television or radio what I've got to say will come over in a very natural way. Looking back on the running debate I had with Robertson's agent, Bill McMurdo, on both television

John Robertson receives a crystal presentation from Hearts to mark his goalscoring feats with the club.

channels as well as radio, I'm surprised that no one was smart enough to wake up to the idea of selling tickets!

Seriously, I do feel that I have a responsibility to open up the cupboards of the club for the media, and if that occasionally means rattling a few skeletons, then I'm quite prepared to take the bad with the indifferent and the good. There is no doubt whatsoever that I enjoy media attention, and I would be the first to admit that there have been times, particularly in the early days, when I went a little over the top. But at least the supporters know where the buck stops, and that my involvement with the media is a means to an end, namely to use publicity as a tool to improve the lot of our spectators and our players.

Just as the position of Hearts has improved since the early 1980s, so the picture in Scotland generally has become more buoyant. The SFA has never been healthier, the supporters – both in a domestic and an international context – have cleaned their act up, and apart from one or two isolated incidents the players have also done their part. In short, everyone has worked hard to improve the status and the image of the industry.

We can't allow all that endeavour to be frittered away by failing to maintain our initiative. That's why I reacted personally the day that Mark Walters made his first appearance for Rangers at Tynecastle. The first major black footballer to compete in the Premier Division, Walters was the subject of racist taunts and fruit-throwing. Although I was advised to stay out of the matter, I reacted like an angry customer. I approached the club secretary, Les Porteous, and told him that an announcement should be put over the tannoy in my name saying that such behaviour had to stop immediately.

It used to be the case at Tynecastle that those in command adopted a policy of keeping their heads under the barricades whenever the flak started to fly. That's not my way, and I remember a time a number of years ago when Motherwell were the visitors to Tynecastle for a match that would decide whether or not we gained promotion to the Premier Division. Trouble broke out on the terracing and there was the appalling sight of policemen being carried away injured. I got out of my seat in the directors' box and walked round to where the trouble was to see if I could be of any use in quelling the disturbance. It was a most sobering afternoon for me – we lost the match and didn't win promotion, though in the long run that was probably a good thing for the club – and if it was a low point in my time with Hearts, at least it rammed home the message of how much frustration was felt by our supporters.

I had no idea until I took that short walk that afternoon of the extent of the anger and the sense of disappointment that was emanating from the terracings at Tynecastle. Of course nothing could justify the reaction that led to policemen being carried away (today we endeavour to keep police and supporters on opposite sides of the perimeter fencing). But for me the day had value in that I came face to face with the bitterness that lay behind some of our off-the-field problems. Having confronted the power that lay on the terracings, I knew we had to keep it under control and, hopefully, in time channel that energy into a more positive backing for the team. That's why I believe there is a direct correlation between what happens on the pitch and what happens on the terracing. If you have undisciplined players, how can you expect the supporters to behave themselves? I've always taken a stand against bigotry of any description, and think that players who make gestures or cross themselves are acting in a provocative manner. We must never forget that we are dealing with a tinder-box situation. There was speculation after the aforementioned match with Rangers that Hugh Burns was cautioned for an alleged remark made to Mark Walters. Whatever the merits of that speculation, Burns was severely warned by me, and the point made in no uncertain terms that this club will not stand for any form of intolerance.

As a personal view, I believe that standards are set in a football club by the relationship between the chairman and the management. In other words it starts at the top, and that is the axis around which everything else revolves. You must have discipline, respect and control from the management down. That is an absolutely fundamental prerequisite and sets the tone for the players and the supporters.

A small example of the importance of discipline at Tynecastle may be enough to illustrate my point. Early in 1988 a couple of Hearts players fell out over some incident during a match, and one of the pair made a gesture which went unseen by the vast majority of the crowd and was not reported at any stage by the Press. However, Alex MacDonald and Sandy Jardine saw what happened and the player concerned was fined £300 and given a stern talking-to as to his future conduct by the club. The simple fact of the matter was that a highly paid member of staff had not behaved in a professional manner and had to be reminded of his responsibilities.

Not adhering to professional conduct was also what lay behind the initial public disagreement between John Robertson and Hearts. I was quite willing originally to give the player the chance to clear the air by asking him whether or not his agent was touting him around France.

But when I walked into a board meeting I was shown a newspaper article, clearly precipitated by the player's agent, saying "Pay up or I go". Now whether or not Robertson actually said that is an irrelevance, because the agent was promoting that viewpoint and was happy to have it said. The headline made the point, and given that our players, like everyone else, read the sports pages, we had no option but to make it clear that Robertson could not be singled out for special treatment. All we could do at that point was show Robertson the door.

You've got to be prepared to take the rough with the smooth when you are in the public eye, but there's no doubt in my mind that, other than the club's supporters, the media has been my biggest ally during the rebuilding of Hearts. I think I can say in all honesty that during the past seven years I've never fallen out with a journalist over a story. And there's only been one occasion when I wrote to an editor to complain about something.

At Tynecastle we like to regard ourselves as an honest, open club. We don't pick and choose our friends in the media. Indeed, I think that by and large football in Scotland is fortunate to attract such a high standard of journalism. Of course there are times when sensational headlines do distort the facts, but I understand the pressure on the tabloids to come up with a never-ending stream of new angles. And, over the piece, the coverage is excellent.

Given that I would hope the media will show us an interest when we have something to promote, equally if there is dirty washing on the line then there is no way that we can run for cover. In my view it is important to be available for the stories that may not suit you as well as the ones that do. In the early days I was more prone to going over the top than I am now, and it was the counsel of experienced journalists that helped me to learn the rules of the game. Once you know the ropes – and having tantrums after matches about referees, for instance, is never a very clever tactic – you can duck and weave and make your point without landing yourself on the floor.

Having been relatively successful in other areas of business before getting involved as a club chairman, it still came as a surprise just how powerful a marketing tool a football club can be. As a supporter of football for years I'd read the back pages of the newspapers like everyone else, but until becoming involved personally it was hard to take in the sheer scale of the thing. The attention, for instance, that was paid at the Press conference to announce my introduction at Tynecastle was nothing short of staggering.

From the beginning I felt that if I was going to take the business of running Hearts forward, then I would need to tap into the goodwill that exists towards football. I would like to think that over the years I've helped to create not only a position and a status for Hearts, but also made some sort of impression on those with an interest in football as an honest trader. I'm arrogant enough to believe that the public see me differently from what might be described as the fuddy-duddies in the game. I'm not one of those faceless wonders who never venture an opinion if they can help it and seem to regard football as akin to a private club where members only are welcome. I prize the position I have with Hearts and it is something that I work at.

The media has been my biggest ally during the rebuilding of Hearts. Here I discuss the situation with media mogul, Robert Maxwell.

Although I am a person who does react to things off the cuff, equally I give careful consideration to what I have to say, because I want to reach not just the supporters who follow Hearts, but all those with an interest in the game. That's why I feel a sense of responsibility in my dealings with the Press. On that topic, it always disappoints me when I hear of situations arising where the power of cheque-book journalism holds sway. I would never allow any of my employees at Tynecastle to sign a contract with a specific newspaper. I'm dead set against such arrangements, because in my book they inevitably mean that you don't afford the rest similar access. Regardless of who was the manager at Tynecastle, he would not be allowed to do a deal of that nature. I think the Press are entitled to an even shake – and, of course, it was also in the interests of the club to reach as broad an audience as possible.

Perhaps I'm more fortunate than many other people in football in that I've had a chance to host my own television programme on BBC Scotland as well as a long-running chat show on Radio Forth. Not only did those programmes help me to meet a lot of interesting folk; they also improved my ability to run my business. And when you're asking the questions rather than answering them, you're coming at a subject from the other side of the glass and appreciating the problems that a professional encounters in putting light and shade into a decent piece of work.

My final guest in the second series of the Wallace Mercer hour – Malcolm Rifkind, the Secretary of State for Scotland, 27 Nov. 1987.

I've been asked if I give people too much access because I never refuse to take a call from anyone in the media. Even when it is inconvenient to me I will always try to be of as much assistance as I can. I value the relationship I have with numerous journalists and they know me well enough to understand that we share a common ground of mutual respect and the public's right to know.

CHAPTER SIXTEEN

Taking Stock

WALLACE MERCER

I N ORDER TO ASSESS the quality and organisation of the game in Scotland today, and how it relates to what is happening in England and Europe, it is worth while to go back to the beginning of the 1980s when many of the big city clubs, most notably Hearts, struggled to cope with the punitive 20 per cent failure rate imposed by a ten-club Premier Division that relegated two of its members each year.

When I bought the Tynecastle club in 1981, Hearts were caught in a vicious trap – too good for the First Division but not good enough for the Premier Division. This brought about the "yo-yo" syndrome where the club bounced up and down between the two Divisions for the best part of a decade.

As a businessman coming into football, I regarded the failure rate in the Premier Division as unacceptably high. In spite of what people may think, I don't see myself as being in the risk business. I am an investor in football, and at that stage the way the League was set up, the future of a club like Hearts was in jeopardy, at least to some extent, because of forces beyond its control.

The number one priority of the Premier Division must be to maintain football players in full-time employment. And, within reason, it is clearly prudent to provide a set-up in which the best stadia are put to the fullest use. There should also be a centralisation of power and resources in the hands of those clubs capable of attracting and maintaining the status of the game. In short, from my angle a failure rate of two out of ten was too fraught with danger. It was also the case that clubs with a smaller economic base were able to tilt at windmills to some extent and keep the larger clubs out, though due credit must be given to clubs like Partick Thistle and Morton who seemed to be able to manage the business of surviving in the top ten better than a side like Hearts.

However, it was an unsatisfactory state of affairs from the point of view of the well-being of the Scottish game. Some of the clubs best placed to maintain full-time football, like Hearts, Hibs and Dundee, were the ones suffering most. And if the continuing future of full-time football was in a precarious position, what kind of competition would there be at a future date for the Rangers and Celtics of the League? I was quite determined, when I first came into Scottish football, that such a state of affairs could not be allowed to continue. There had to be change. As a newcomer, however, it was not my place to put the match under the bonfire. It was a case of waiting for the catalyst.

There are many people who regard Wallace Mercer as being too outspoken. But in the end I was only so candid because my primary ambition was to consolidate Hearts in the Premier Division. Also, I was keen that the money I had put into the club would be guaranteed in the future. To be blunt, I had no intention of investing huge sums of money in Hearts for the sake of playing football in the First Division. In my estimation such a projection spelled economic suicide. Thus, in my first two or three years with Hearts I worked extra hard at culturing as positive a response as I could from the market.

I make no bones about the fact that it was to the benefit of Hearts when the whole issue concerning the power base of the game came to a head a couple of years ago. It was at that point that an awareness amongst the leading clubs – and Hearts were not in that category at that stage – crystallised into a desire for change. Chris Anderson, then the vice-chairman of Aberdeen but sadly no longer with us, had done much to precipitate the debate. Chris was one of the prime forces behind the introduction of the Premier Division in the first place. He appreciated better than most that additional change was needed to ensure the continuing well-being of full-time football in Scotland.

In many ways I looked at what Aberdeen had achieved and regarded the Pittodrie club as a role model for Hearts. Chris had been to America to look at the way professional sport was organised there, and he held the view that in an ideal world, if you were starting from scratch you would organise Scottish football on a franchise basis. Under the circumstances that prevailed in the real world, such an outcome was unlikely, to say the least. However, the debate that surrounded the issue of live television coverage helped to bring matters to a head. The actual question of television's involvement, paradoxically, was not that crucial in itself. But by that stage I was well acquainted with Dick Donald, Tom Devlin and John Paton, the respective chairmen of Aberdeen, Celtic and Rangers, and ours was a coming together of like minds.

The other bone of contention was the fact that the smaller clubs could control the management of the Premier Division and, for that matter, the economic fortunes of the leading clubs. All told, it was an intolerable state of affairs. The first meeting of the disaffected clubs took place in the boardroom at Tynecastle, and it was with some delight that Hearts played a strong role in the drama that unfolded.

In retrospect, I have to say that if I had had my way we would have taken matters to their ultimate conclusion. Having made it clear that we were prepared to break away and form our own league, I believe we should have stuck to our guns rather than cobbling together an unhappy compromise. I think that state of affairs came about partly because of certain changes that took place at Rangers FC around this time. Having gone so far down the road and yet fallen short of what we wanted to achieve, we were left with a 12-club Premier Division which for three seasons cast a malign spell over the game. True, it generated more revenue, but the sheer volume of games was bad news for the spectators as well as for the players, who picked up a staggering number of injuries. On top of that the quality of play declined, and that put pressure on our international team, which is the shop window for Scottish football. And, in European competition, there was the classic example of Dundee United's marvellous run in the UEFA Cup being undone at the last hurdle by weary legs.

This season, happily, we've returned to a ten-club Premier Division with just one club relegated. Should I achieve nothing else as an investor in Scottish football, at least I've been part of that change. Given the drop in the failure rate from 20 per cent to ten per cent, Hearts will never get themselves into the kind of mess again where the club could be relegated.

Mark you, this season we'll play eight fewer League matches and revenue will drop. I just hope that clubs have estimated their budgets for the season properly and erred on the side of caution. That's another reason why clubs needed to be prudent when it came to renewing the players' contracts this year. It is a mistake to assume that 1989 will necessarily be another bonanza year. Hearts were cautious, and it will be interesting to see if others took the same judicious view.

There have also been changes behind the scenes in the power base of the game, and the structure is now fundamentally different. The big clubs will no longer find themselves outvoted by the smaller clubs when it comes to matters related to their own needs. I regard myself as a supporter of the smaller clubs because I'm fully aware of the need below the top level for a thriving grass-roots industry. But it would be wrong to pretend that the major priority lies anywhere other than with the big battalions. The top clubs must have the economic clout and the quality players. If we are not to get the best out of our most talented footballers, then it is common sense not to overplay them.

The bigger clubs eventually achieved the minimum that was required to go about their business in an effective manner. However, I would have to say that in the event of that position being threatened in the future, we would be bound to go back to some sort of breakaway scenario. The status quo in Scotland makes adequate provision for a club like Hearts, but I don't see the current situation as the final chapter in what will always be an unfolding tale. In the last analysis, it is not what I want as the chairman at Tynecastle that matters, nor is it what the administrators may or may not think is good for football. It is what the public wants – and they are the ones who will dictate the shape of future markets.

There is also the question of the needs and wishes of corporate sponsors. Their thoughts turn more and more to exposure on television or video or satellite, and in many respects that visual consideration will have an increasing bearing on the future of Scottish football.

If I was asked to look into a crystal ball and try and predict where we'll be in five or ten years' time, I can see a British Cup, a British League and even a European League down the road. The European League would involve a regional break-up of clubs, but as members of the EEC in an age where jet travel has shrunk distances, there is no reason why barriers shouldn't come down. As a businessman, it is no more difficult for me to fly to Amsterdam than it is to Manchester. What, then, is to prevent football teams commuting across similar distances on a more regular basis than they do in the present Cup competitions? Why shouldn't Hearts be part of a future plan where Ajax, PSV Eindhoven and Bordeaux are regular ports of call? The whole picture will change in the years ahead, and perhaps the process of reform will take place more rapidly than many fully appreciate at the moment.

At any rate, as things stand here and now, I would have to say that Hearts have cordial relations with both the Scottish League and the

Scottish Football Association and that both those organisations do a
good job. In particular, the SFA is an extremely well-run, professional
body that secretary Ernie Walker and his colleagues have transformed
into one of the most businesslike national associations in Europe.

People have talked disparagingly about Ernie Walker as the Ayatollah
of the Scottish game – but credit where credit is due. The man has
pulled the SFA up by its bootlaces and earned us respect throughout
the football world for the progress that has been made both in the field
of coaching and in attempting to clean up the game's act. Equally,
under the guidance of Jim Farry at the League, we've had an adequate
performance in recent seasons. I believe that the power block of larger
clubs should assist the Scottish League's secretary in administering the
League's arrangements.

In the future, however, I can envisage a time when domestic national
associations and international bodies such as UEFA and FIFA will
have   much   closer   links.   I'm   not   making   any   particular
recommendations on this topic but what I say is this: the big clubs are
now run by businessmen and carry such a high level of investment that
we must act together on the basis of what is best for us as a group. We
have a relationship and a common philosophy which will ensure a unity
of purpose in the future that was not always evident in the past.

When you looked across the football map of Europe last season from
Real Madrid in Spain to PSV Eindhoven in Holland to Liverpool in
England, the gap between the best and the also-rans had once more
increased. To survive, football at the top level must be competitive and
the public, the sponsors and television will all insist on new ways of
staging the very best matches. I don't regard myself as an investor solely
in the Scottish game. I am an investor in European football. There are
many others like-minded and that is why it is not a case of *if* change will
come, but *when*.

For a variety of reasons, I was absolutely delighted when the
Lawrence Group made their commitment in buying Rangers. They
went from being a minority investor to being the club's owners and
transformed Rangers in the process. What we've seen in the last couple
of years at Ibrox has been the Americanisation of running a football
club in Britain.

To a certain extent I think Rangers have borrowed some of their
corporate ideas from the things we'd done at Tynecastle. The change
was to use that business philosophy and board structure and apply it on
a bigger scale. Overall, what's happened at Ibrox has been good news
for the business of Scottish football. More power to their elbow as far as

I'm concerned, though it was absolutely vital that the other leading clubs reacted to what was happening with Rangers. On the field of play we had to show not only that we could live with them, but also that we could beat them.

No matter how much cash you pour into a team there are no guarantees in football. I've been through the scenario myself and I'm sure David Holmes and Lawrence Marlborough appreciate the point. No one coming into football can work from the starting position that money equals success. All that cash can do is give you the opportunity of employing the best professionals. You still have to put a team together on and off the field. Having said all that, it would actually have been bad news for Rangers' business if they'd run away with all the domestic honours last season after taking the title in Graeme Souness's first year as manager. Without the ingredient of competition everyone's gates will tail off.

There are some who criticise the Premier Division as an overly competitive league that doesn't maintain a high enough standard of player discipline. I don't go along with that line of thinking. You have to keep in mind that football is a segment of the entertainment industry and the publicity machine likes to throw up villains as well as heroes. Personally, I don't think there are any more villains in football than in any other team sport. Let's face it, the game can't survive wholly on a diet of sweetness and light. Most of the supposed darker element is good, knockabout stuff that helps to sell newspapers and puts a few bottoms on seats.

It is up to each club to impose a standard of discipline. As I've said elsewhere in the book, I regard the relationship between the chairman and the management team as absolutely fundamental in setting the tone for the conduct of the team. You have to strike a balance between wanting to win and the desire to win at all costs. This is where the responsibility rests with the chairman and the manager. A decision has to be taken on the line you will cross and the line you won't cross. I know where that line, both on a business and a personal level, exists at Tynecastle. There are things we wouldn't do just for a piece of silverware or a flag.

I've spoken in the past about our refereeing standards in Scotland, and once raised the issue of the pros and cons of professionalism. As things stand today, I believe there should be a circuit of high-quality referees who specialise in handling the top matches. It must be terribly difficult at the moment for a referee to handle a Second Division game in one week and then be thrown into the cauldron of a top Premier

Division match the next. My view is that there are key contests drawing huge numbers of paying customers that carry extra pressure and require the handling of our most able officials. You need the fittest and most aware referees in order to do justice to the teams fielding the best players in the game where there is most at stake.

There is no reason why the top referee shouldn't command a higher fee than colleagues with less responsibility. This is not the same thing as arguing for full-time professionals. It is simply to note that, as in other walks of life, excellence should be rewarded.

I wouldn't say that our game is handled by amateurs, because our referees are of a pretty good standard. But there is room for improvement. The more former players we can attract into refereeing after their playing days are over, the better. Ex-players would not only bring an understanding of the rules, but also first-hand experience of the kind of pressure that the leading teams are under.

CHAPTER SEVENTEEN

Business Class

WALLACE MERCER

SCOTTISH FOOTBALL was on the rocks at the start of the decade. The hooligan element off the field was out of control and new legislation was required to curb the presence of alcohol in the grounds as well as to give the police more power to control supporters. It was on this foundation of sanity on the terracings that subsequent strides forward on the field of play and in the boardrooms of the leading clubs were firmly based.

When I joined Hearts in 1981 the club was financially insolvent and within weeks of closure. For ten years Hearts, to all intents and purposes, had been operated and run by the Bank of Scotland. The board of directors were notionally in charge of the team's affairs, but every time the overdraft reached a certain point the only response was to sell another player. Inevitably, what happened next was that the well ran dry – and there were no more players to sell. Previous administrations of this club didn't have control over their costs. Aspects of running a football club such as police charges and rates, with high fixed costs, were allowed to get out of control. Meantime the number of supporters attending matches were an ever-dwindling group. Indeed, when I took over, Hearts had just managed to go through a season in the Premier Division with a total home gate of 125,000. By comparison, in the 1987/88 football year almost 450,000 customers came to Tynecastle to watch matches.

Those figures give some indication of the growth of interest in the activities of Hearts during my seven years at Tynecastle. To begin with, when the club was in the First Division, we faced enormous problems. Hearts found themselves in a position where revenue was reduced even further. We remained a full-time outfit during those dark days even though it was impossible to fund the cost of that commitment from income earned at the gate.

The first thing I had to do was to cut back the backroom staff. The management of the playing side was unaffected, but the physiotherapy department went, the secretarial personnel were pruned, and the players had to take reductions in salary. The basic wage was set at a low level and the bonuses for winning were dramatically increased. It was crystal clear to me that only when the team started to win would the fortunes of the club begin to take a turn for the better.

In 1981/82 I spent around £400,000 on new players, which for a club in our position was a substantial investment. I also contributed interest-free loans in excess of £100,000 and other directors also made significant sums available. There are still players on our staff who were acquired as a direct result of the personal funding of the board.

In short, our genesis was humble indeed. The management team of Alex MacDonald and Sandy Jardine learned their apprenticeship during the years in the First Division. The only seam of gold that came with the territory in those days was the shining talent of John Robertson, David Bowman and Gary Mackay. All three players were signed for the club by Bobby Moncur as teenagers. In due course Bowman and Robertson were to leave Tynecastle, and their going raised the best part of £1 million for Hearts.

However, those transfers have been the only substantial sales Hearts have been involved in during seven years. I appreciated from the start that the only way out of the trap the club was in was to break the vicious circle of debt and outgoing transfers. When David Bowman went to Coventry for £180,000 his departure helped to bring in some capital, though it was also clear at the time that the player himself needed a change. John Robertson's case was different. When Newcastle came in with a bid of £750,000 we felt that the money would help us restructure the team. MacDonald and Jardine had always been good purchasers of players when money was tight, and after Robertson's departure I felt obliged to make the cash available that would assist us to add quality to the team in a number of positions.

As Hearts have got their act together over the past seven years, so has Scottish football as a whole. There is a direct correlation between the two, and I'd like to think that we've been in the vanguard of a number of changes for the better. Ironically, the absence of English clubs from Europe probably helped our cause because it enabled Premier Division sides to attract top individuals from the Football League to earn their living north of the border.

Guests on Wallace Mercer's Friends *show broadcast on BBC Scotland Television on 19 March 1988 – James Gulliver, Body Shop's Anita Roddick and Sir Clive Sinclair.*

Football is like any other business: competition begets competition; and competition begets demand. If you walk down any high street and discover four antique shops grouped together, that hasn't happened by accident. You might wonder why they weren't spaced out around the town. The fact of the matter is that people who go to antique shops will be attracted to the area where there is the greatest choice. It is the same in the football industry. Those at the top thrive on the competition of their closest rivals. However, a gap is opening up between the leading group and the rest, who are increasingly on the fringe of things.

As the image of the Scottish game has improved, so has the support from the sponsors grown. We were among the first in Scotland to introduce shirt sponsorship. There were other innovative ideas like building restaurants and club entertainment facilities that have also been successfully copied elsewhere. In the present economic climate it is not possible to keep the show on the road just through gate income alone. When we sell season tickets to our supporters I remind them that if it wasn't for the help we get from wealthy businessmen, shirt sponsors and other related commercial activities, the cost to the working man to watch football would be so much higher. And at Tynecastle we are very much aware of trying to make it as cheap as possible for ordinary people to come here and support their team.

On that point, I should stress that Hearts are different from a number of other competitors in that the football club is not run as a subsidiary of my business. It has never been looked after in that way for the benefit of Pentland Securities Ltd. The club has been managed as a social investment. I explain this point because none of us have taken any capital out of the business since we put the money in during 1981. Hearts are not controlled for the benefit of Wallace Mercer. It is my view that football clubs cannot entirely be run as profit centres. If that was ever to be the case, then important aspects like fellowship and sportsmanship would disappear out the window. In other words, I will use all the business techniques I can and make best use of our situation in Scotland's capital city to help my football club. But what matters most is the players and the supporters; the business element comes after that.

As the largest shareholder of a public company, I'm willing to bet that if I put it to the shareholders – "Do you want a pretty balance sheet or a team that wins things?" – the response of most of the 750 share-holders will be, "To heck with the balance sheet and just go out and win the Cup or the League". At the same time, the reality of life is that there has to be an even-handed approach. I still give this club personal support in terms of guaranteeing bank facilities. So that helps me to keep a perspective between the emotional side and the business context.

In the last seven years Hearts have become one of the most financially sound football clubs in Britain. We've made a trading profit for the past six years. And at the time of writing, the club had no debts and assets involving the team and the stadium worth approximately £6 million.

Since 1981 we've spent something like £2.5 million on new talent and in the region of £750,000 on improvements to our stadium. All these positive developments have been achieved thanks to the revenue we've earned and the commercial support we've enlisted. During this time it has become ever more apparent to me – and I make no apology for stressing the point again – that you can have the best managers, the best directors, the best commercial department, but it all counts for nothing if you don't have the players. My job, put quite simply, is to give the management team of MacDonald and Jardine the best group of players we can afford.

Dave McPherson, one of Hearts' big buys.

Of course, it would be quite wrong to make the assumption that there is an enormous well of potential resources just waiting to be tapped. Rangers have a deal with Scottish Brewers that is quite unique in scale. The rest of us have to go into the market-place, and it is vital in that context that we continue to nurture and protect the image of our game. I don't just mean the public relations image, but the way our managers behave, the way our players behave and the onus on directors to maintain the emphasis on the suitability of the game as a spectacle for a family audience.

Having broken the ice and attracted major companies to invest in football, we can't afford to sit back and become casual about the situation. It was excellent news when Barclay's replaced *Today* as the sponsors of the Football League because that lent the game credibility. It showed that football wasn't just there to sell a Japanese television set or a newspaper or whatever. Here we had a large international bank choosing to put some money into the sport. Psychologically it was a boost for everyone.

In Scotland we have to bear in mind that unless the influx of sponsorship is handled correctly it will all disappear just as quickly as it arrived. And the consequences of such unbusinesslike behaviour would be serious indeed.

Like many things in life, football doesn't stand still. We have to be aware and ready to deal with changes that affect us. As far as the transfer market is concerned, we are going to have to think long and hard in the not-too-distant future about the amount of money we are prepared to invest in players. When Newcastle bought John Robertson from us for around £750,000 at the time that was a record transfer fee for the St James's Park club. Yet they already had on their books the Brazilian superstar, Mirandinha, for under £600,000. How did this come about?

The simple answer is that market forces outwith the United Kingdom dictate that quality players are available at a cheaper price. Although there was speculation that Robertson would have attracted considerable interest on the Continent, the fact that his fee would have been dictated by a formula of ten times salary would have ensured the player carried the kind of price tag that would have enabled a French or West German club to purchase a native internationalist. This trend is sure to continue. It is already clear that by 1992 the mobility of labour encouraged by the Treaty of Rome will, to all intents and purposes, cancel transfer fees altogether.

Those of us currently involved in putting money into long-term contracts for players are going to have to watch our step. The fact of the matter is that in future, if there is going to be a fee at all for a player, it will be greatly reduced compared to the present market. And, of course, the adjunct to that is that we will have to pay out far larger signing-on fees and much higher wages to attract a decent calibre of player. The tragedy of this situation will not so much affect clubs at the top of the heap. We will still have a large income from our gates and draw substantially from sponsorship. The clubs that will suffer most are those in the lower reaches who rely on trading players in order to balance the books. This applies on both sides of the border. Inevitably it will mean that the gulf between the haves and the have-nots will increase yet again.

It is out of this financial situation, as I've argued elsewhere, that a different structure for the game will emerge. I foresee in the long term a variety of European leagues in which the clubs of matching economic resources will band together. By then the barriers of parochialism will have been dismantled. That would lead to a market with three or four tiers of competitiveness. And I appreciate that we would not be able to compete with the Barcelonas, the Real Madrids and the Liverpools. However, we would be in a position to hold our own with just about anyone else.

This process of international fragmentation will take many years to evolve. In order to cope with what lies ahead it will be imperative to have economic strength. That's why I envisage amalgamations between clubs and the rationalisation of our industry.

Through all this change in the way the business is run, however, the status of the player will, if anything, be enhanced. I think that the modern player does a superb job. He deserves every penny of whatever salary he makes in the course of a short and demanding career. We tend only to pay attention to those at the glamorous end of the business, whose job is winning trophies and representing their country. But it is the other 95 per cent of players who make up the bulk of the industry, and for them it is anything but a glamorous life. The rewards may be slightly higher than in the workplace outwith the game, but for the average player with a family it is no better than an adequate living from a sport that carries the underlying risk of serious injury.

It was one of the themes of my speech to the Scottish Football Writers' Dinner in Glasgow in May 1988 that there is a need for a much stronger players union. That organisation needs to protect the broad mass of their membership, and not just the interests of the superstars. Having said that, it is only right and proper that the best command the greatest remuneration. If I felt as an owner that a player was bringing extra people through the gate and proving a significant draw as a personality, then the sky would be the limit as regards salary to keep that individual. Putting backsides on seats is what it is all about, and we would be willing to pay huge money to the right player.

In fact, I would go so far as to say that as long as I am at Tynecastle no one will ever leave for financial reasons unless I want them to go. It shouldn't be overlooked that there is a fair amount of wealth on the Hearts board. I'm supposed to be a multimillionaire, and Douglas Park is also worth millions. We are not just paper tigers. There is a degree of personal wealth round our boardroom table as well as the club's own resources. What I'm saying is that we are businessmen, and you don't cut your own throat by letting someone go if his talent helps you to run your business.

Overall, I think that there are a lot of good, young, bright minds organising our sport as we head towards the 1990s. David Stein at Arsenal, Irving Scholar at Spurs and Martin Edwards at Manchester United have all been successes in other areas, and now apply their expertise in football.

In Scotland there is the example of what Lawrence Marlborough has done at Ibrox, and I've already complimented the changes at Rangers elsewhere. And we shouldn't overlook that sharp cookie at Pittodrie, the Aberdeen chairman Dick Donald, who has lasted the pace so well. To some extent what has taken place at Tynecastle was modelled on the pattern set at Aberdeen by Dick Donald and Chris Anderson. I couldn't pay Dick a greater compliment than to note that as a former professional dancer, he could still show the young lions a step or two.

CHAPTER EIGHTEEN

Chairman's Report

WALLACE MERCER

I N MY PRIVATE moments immediately after the defeat from Celtic in the semi-final of the Scottish Cup at Hampden, I had to look at myself as leader of the football club. I had to ask myself whether or not I had the nervous energy, the commitment and the drive to take another emotional battering like the one we suffered that day.

There was never any lingering question that I would quit as chairman, but at the same time I knew that certain decisions would have to be made and that there would need to be a recasting of personnel. I don't think, either, that there was any question of my fellow directors wanting me to step down as chairman; but from a personal point of view, if I didn't feel the appetite, the urgency and the hunger to get the club to the top, then I simply wouldn't be prepared to carry on.

I then looked at my management team of Alex MacDonald and Sandy Jardine, two well-paid men with excellent jobs. I had to think about their positions too. MacDonald and Jardine have both given superb service to Hearts, but I had to consider the effect of the traumatic defeat on them. In fact I was even more convinced after that afternoon of great disappointment for the club that the will and the desire to succeed was more deeply ingrained in Jardine and MacDonald than ever before. It wasn't something I even discussed with them. But the more the management and the players get knocked down, the more they want to bounce back. That's how I feel too.

One of the decisions that were made in the aftermath of Hampden concerned the future of our centre-forward, John Robertson. The departure of Robertson to Newcastle United for a fee of around £750,000 was one of the most significant events for us in the course of the 1987/88 season. I had been down the contract road twice before with John and his agent, Bill McMurdo. I knew there was bound to be speculation about the player's future, and no one at Tynecastle was in any doubt that the number one priority as far as John was concerned was to secure financial security for his family. As the club's top scorer for a number of years, and as a young man with an ambition to play in English football, there was no debate either that John was a marketable commodity.

Negotiations between Hearts and John Robertson over a new contract were always going to be fraught with difficulty. In the time that had elapsed since John signed a deal two years previously other players in our squad had made significant progress and achieved even higher status in the game than our centre-forward. It is my view that, on a subconscious level at least, John wanted to get away from Hearts because he wasn't being considered for a place on the international scene when three members of our team – Gary Mackay, John Colquhoun and Henry Smith – had already won caps.

There was never going to be a scenario where I was prepared to offer John a huge deal in order to persuade him to sign another contract with us. The fact of the matter was that if I'd done that for him, then I'd also have been duty-bound to make similar offers to our three full internationalists.

It could have been that John thought he was more special to us than I regarded him, and, although it wasn't the deciding factor in the matter, John has a consistent problem with his weight. That is something which goes along with his physical make-up. Our worry was that in the event of securing a highly attractive contract with us over the next three years, the motivation might not have been there on John's part to keep his weight under control. When you're talking about a forward who needs to be both sharp and mobile, pounds rather than stones can make a difference.

Around the time that Newcastle United came on the scene and made us an offer in the region of £750,000, we felt that the bid was a fair price for the player and avoided the necessity of having to go to a tribunal to fix a valuation. All the elements had to be balanced, of course. We knew that on the basis of John's earnings the club would still have received almost £600,000 from a Continental tribunal. John was a well-paid player at Tynecastle, and one of the reasons he was so highly rewarded was to protect the club in the event of the player exercising freedom of contract and a tribunal being called in.

That's how it came about that the day we lost to Celtic at Hampden in the semi-final of the Scottish Cup was the one that I decided the first team needed to be reconstructed. If Robertson moved on, then I could give my management team of Alex MacDonald and Sandy Jardine real money to spend for the first time in their careers. What we got from Newcastle for Robertson, plus the cash the club already had put aside, meant that there was almost £1 million available to invest in new players.

Until the deal was done it was a very upsetting time for everyone at the club. Robertson's agent, Bill McMurdo, had the temerity to ask for a signing-on fee of £100,000 and wages of £1,000 a week. Whatever Robertson and McMurdo say to the contrary now, their manipulation of the popular press was putting pressure on us and could be seen to be causing problems in the dressing-room. The one thing we have at Tynecastle that I would do everything in my power to preserve, and that I will not allow to be broken by outsider interference, is our sense of togetherness.

Given all these different factors, I went to the managers after the defeat by Celtic and told them that I thought we should seriously consider selling John Robertson if the right offer came along. I know that as far as many of our supporters were concerned John was very much the favourite son, and his contribution to the fortunes of Hearts as a consistent goalscorer will always be held in high esteem. In many respects his move to Tyneside will either be the making or the breaking of him. It goes without saying that we wish him well.

In conclusion, I would say that if things don't work out for John in England, then we would be absolutely delighted to have him back. As I said, he is a favourite son of this club, and while I understand he feels the need to savour English football, there will always be a welcome for him at Tynecastle. Given the money Newcastle have paid for John, they're expecting a star, and I have to say that a shiver went down my spine when Willie McFaul described the player as the new Kevin Keegan. John has many attributes, the most significant of which is his ability to score goals, but it seemed to me an unfair burden on the lad to draw comparisons with a footballer of a quite different calibre.

There are those who subscribe to the view that I manipulated the entire situation with John Robertson so that the club secured a substantial transfer fee without attracting the bad publicity that usually accompanies the departure of top players. In fact none of it was preplanned. What I will say, though, is that I devoted more mental energy to the public performance of that particular escapade than anything else between Act One in February and the Final Curtain in April when the cheque was banked!

The matter required daily attention, and while my primary responsibility was to my players, I also had to consider how the market was going to react. The acid test of that at the end of season 1987/88 was that we took in more money from season ticket sales in 1988 than we did in 1987 – and that after selling the individual who was supposed to be our star player.

I worked hard both before and after the sale of Robertson to mark journalists' cards and let them know that we would be spending money on new players. The purpose of that was to ease people into the way of thinking that the team needed to be rebuilt – and that the money from Robertson's transfer was required in order to do it.

By the time John left for St James's Park I no longer regarded him as the club's most saleable asset. I would regard John Colquhoun, an international forward who enjoyed a superb 1987/88 season, as a particularly valuable player. If anyone had asked me at the turn of the year, when it came time to renew a number of contracts, which player I wanted to hang on to most, then John Colquhoun was the man who fitted the bill. His presence off the field as chairman of the Players Union and his flexibility on the pitch made him our primary target for retention. To get John's new deal under wraps in January was the best piece of business I've done this year. Henry Smith, our international goalkeeper, also signed a new long-term deal; and so John Robertson was left in splendid isolation until his move to Newcastle.

It happened to Celtic in 1987 when players like Maurice Johnston and Brian McClair were due to come out of contract, and to a certain extent teams like Aberdeen and ourselves also suffered in 1988 from the end-of-contract syndrome. I think there is a connection between the uncertain, unsettled mood of players off the field and disappointing performances on it. After the whole Robertson business had been the focus of public attention in newspapers, radio and television, we went to Brockville and lost to Falkirk, a defeat which almost certainly scuttled our hope of taking Celtic down to the wire in the Championship.

Funnily enough, it was after that defeat from Falkirk that John Colquhoun approached me and said that he wanted the news of his re-signing to be announced. In fact the contract had been signed months earlier but the details had been held back as a marketing ploy on my part. However, given the harsh words that were being bandied around during the Robertson business, John Colquhoun wanted the Hearts support to know that he was very happy to be staying with the club.

Perhaps there were also underlying tensions in the dressing-room at the time caused by the contractual dispute and that was why, as father of the family at Tynecastle, I had to make the decision that the favourite son had to go. In the end it wasn't about money, because I can honestly offer the assurance that if I had wanted John to stay, he would have been made an offer that would have kept him with us. He would have got his £100,000 signing-on fee and a wage of £1,000 a week. But I didn't value the player's services at that price.

I say again that the only players who will leave this club are the ones that I want to go. I've intentionally used the singular rather than the plural in this instance, because as club chairman and major shareholder I have some influence on these matters.

One player who was not allowed to leave Hearts when one of Britain's biggest clubs made an inquiry and made it clear they were prepared to pay around £750,000 for his services was Craig Levein. At that point he had been voted Scotland's Young Player of the Year for two years running and was very much the jewel in our crown.

Craig had the misfortune to suffer a serious knee injury that kept him out of action for almost a year. When he returned to first-team football he slotted back into the scene as to the manner born. You get an idea of the quality of the lad that in the course of this short spell back in action he was called up by Andy Roxburgh into an international squad. Unfortunately, Craig suffered another reverse last season and had to undergo another operation.

Hopefully we will see Craig back again in due course. It has been a very difficult time for the player and his wife, and at Tynecastle we've done everything we could to make sure the player was looked after properly. We've tried to involve him in other areas of the club's business as well as sending him on a holiday to get away from it all.

When you see what's happened to Craig it makes you appreciate the risks of professional football. When he fell like a pack of cards in the dirt track at Tynecastle against Rangers without another player near him, one could see at least £750,000 turning into nothing. That's the risk business of football. For there's no doubt in my mind that but for these injuries Craig would have been our best and most valuable player.

On a personal level, it isn't always appreciated just how fraught a footballer's career can be with injury difficulties. That's why I made reference to the subject, and the need for decent insurance, in my speech to the Scottish Football Writers' Dinner in Glasgow. That gathering brings together all the different strands of the game – administrators, directors, chairmen, sportswriters, managers and players – and I felt it was important to underline what has been one of the major themes of this book: namely, that our most valuable resource is our players. These are ordinary working-class lads earning a living in what can be a ruthless business. Our players have been overplayed recently in Scotland, and I think it is our responsibility to ensure that the Players Union has adequate finance to protect its members. Under Gordon Taylor in England, the Players Union has done a superb job south of the border. I would like to see the association in Scotland matching that kind of achievement – but it will only become stronger if it is better financed. This may mean levies on television income as well as transfer fees, and if that's what it takes then so be it. As a chairman I firmly believe that those of us involved in running the business of football must work hand in glove with those who play the game for a living.

And as far as caring for injured players is concerned, it isn't just about finding the money to enable someone to have an operation. It is about helping someone through a difficult situation and assisting with their mental rehabilitation as well as the restoration of their physical fitness. One of the reasons we've attracted top professionals to Tynecastle and will continue to do so in the future is because the club is run benevolently and the régime is a caring one. True, it is a competitive environment; and, yes, players have got to fight to get into the team. But we look after everyone within our club, whether it is Craig Levein, or Walter Kidd, or Ian Jardine, who also suffered serious injuries in the last year. It is part of the psychology of the Heart of Midlothian football club that injured players feel as much a part of things as those who are playing on a Saturday. We want our injured players to think good thoughts about their employers, not negative ones.

While a number of big buys have helped to bring new faces to Tynecastle, two of the most pleasant aspects of the last football year were the signings of Terry Christie's son and Alex Young's son, two young men with promising futures in the game. It is always vital to recruit your own talent, and I've stressed elsewhere in this book the value to Hearts of Bobby Moncur's signings of John Robertson, Gary Mackay and Dave Bowman.

We've also made shrewd purchases, thanks to the endeavours of the management team in the lower reaches of the English League. In Mike Galloway we got three players in one, and while he could never be described as a shining star, his determined, honest and flexible approach to the game made him a most worthwhile buy.

That's why, when John Robertson left the club, there wasn't an outcry from the supporters, because they believed and trusted me to reinvest every penny in new players.

Eamonn Bannon was a player we'd been interested in signing throughout the season prior to him joining us. This was because we lacked a senior professional who would be in the team on a regular basis. We also needed a player who was rich in experience of the European club scene as well as having played international football and taken part in the World Cup.

I knew when Alex MacDonald told me that he wanted to buy Eamonn that it was sure to cause many problems. I was certain that Jim McLean, the manager of Dundee United, would over react to the situation – not only because we wanted to sign one of his players, but also due to the fact that we are in direct competition with one another. It was no surprise to me that when Alex rang Jim McLean he was told the player was not available. At any rate an offer was put in, and then we had the subsequent difficult time in the press which culminated in a private meeting between myself and George Fox, the chairman of United, that strove to resolve an increasingly acrimonious dispute.

United had also sent us a two-line note making a cash offer of £500,000 for Gary Mackay. We thought that was meant as establishing a benchmark price for Bannon, who was shortly due out of contract and had told the Tannadice club he intended to move on.

We had had our differences with United in the past, and to some extent this did cause bad blood and spilled over on to the field. In the end my responsibility is to make sure that these matters don't become problems on the field or on the terracings. So I spoke to George Fox, we sorted out our differences, and I apologised to him for not speaking to him in the first place. Within two days we concluded an offer of £225,000 that was acceptable to United.

Now, for a player of 30, who was also given first-rate personal terms. it was a considerable outlay, and people have subsequently said to me that we would have got Bannon for a much lower fee if we'd gone to a tribunal. There may be some merit in that, but I wanted to close a deal to avoid discord spilling over into the new season. It was also important not to put extra pressure on Eamonn.

In the final analysis I valued the relationship between Hearts and Dundee United more than the £25,000 or so we could have saved at a tribunal. I don't think clubs of our status should be seen to be bickering in public and getting involved in slanging matches that can have an effect on the supporters.

We also signed Iain Ferguson from United for a fee that was settled by a tribunal. Iain was another vital part of the jigsaw for us and I'm sure his experience in Europe will be invaluable.

On the business side, the football year for me was also not without its turbulent moments. Mita, a Japanese photocopying firm, had become our shirt sponsors three years previously for a sum – I can now reveal for the first time – of around £100,000. Earning just over £30,000 a year from shirt sponsorship was a reasonable deal for us at that time, but Mita received plenty of notice from Hearts that the club's status had changed dramatically and we would be looking for a more lucrative deal. We were looking for at least three times what had been on offer before. Suffice it to say that Mita waited until the eleventh hour before writing us a letter – unsigned by their general manager in England – to say that we were no longer wanted.

It was a most upsetting business because there was no dialogue between ourselves and Mita. Through a certain newspaper I then made it clear that Hearts jersey was up for sale. This in turn did not please the sponsors, who issued a vitriolic press release that was sent to every newspaper in the country. The gist of the statement was that we were not a good club for a sponsor to be associated with, and that Mita had not received value for money for their investment.

That must have been the sickest joke of the year! While the team that was finishing second in the Premier Division was getting £30,000, Second Division Aston Villa, who won promotion to the First Division in England last season, were getting £120,000 from the same sponsors. With the greatest respect, it is difficult to fathom how anyone could regard the deal they were getting from Hearts at that price as anything other than a bargain.

I decided that I wasn't going to take that rubbish from anyone, and I got in touch with the chairman of Mita in Japan. I also wrote to the Japanese embassy and to Mita's marketing director in Europe. Within 48 hours – although this was not revealed at the time – I received both a telephone call and a letter from the company offering a humble apology. The letter claimed that the remarks had been taken out of context. The international marketing director was willing to fly from Amsterdam to Edinburgh to shake hands in the Tynecastle boardroom to show there were no hard feelings. These facts were all held back at the time from the Scottish media because I didn't want to turn the disagreement into a long-running soap opera.

We had to beat off eight other clubs to sign Iain Ferguson from Dundee United.

I'm sometimes accused of propagating a *Dallas*-style public relations exercise at Tynecastle, but this was one instance where enough was enough and there was no need for me to mount a sequel. It was a sad business. But at the end of the day we'd outgrown our old sponsors and were ready to move on to pastures new. Mind you, I don't think Mita appreciated they were taking on Henry Cooper when they had a go at me!

In the changing world of the football business, I'm convinced that agents will have an ever more significant role to play. This was another topic I touched on in my speech to the Scottish Football Writers' Dinner when I began by saying that a strong Players Union might dissuade some players from the necessity of going to an agent. The reality of life is that agents are only likely to be interested in the big earners. This is not meant as a criticism of Bill McMurdo or anyone else. Indeed, to be fair to McMurdo, during the Robertson saga he did well for his client and was quite straight in his dealings with us.

What I do believe, though, is that agents in this country, as happens under UEFA rules on the Continent, should be subject to some sort of self-regulatory body. From our point of view there is no great difference between a business agent, a lawyer or an accountant – we are prepared to deal with anyone at Tynecastle. But it does seem to me no more than common sense that there should be a set of trading standards. The agents themselves, just like insurance brokers and estate agents, might find it is in their own interests to set up something along these lines. At the moment agents are the only part of the football industry that doesn't have a reference point to the authorities.

There is no doubt that agents are here to stay and, if anything, their importance will increase because of great mobility of labour and the legislation contained in the Treaty of Rome. The fact of the matter is that by 1992 players will be able to move freely from one country to another without restriction. And if we must have agents, then I'd rather see former players getting involved than those with no background in the game.

Whatever the hiccups along the way, there was no doubt that the 1987/88 football year was the most successful business-wise since I assumed control of the club in 1981. For the sixth year running we produced a profit, which for a public limited company in the football industry must be a record. Hearts had money in the bank for the first time in seven years, and we were in a position to give substantial funds to our management team to recruit new players. On the playing side we've got three internationalists in our ranks – Henry Smith, Gary Mackay and John Colquhoun – and we finished second to Celtic in the Premier Division. At the turnstiles we enjoyed the best gates we've ever had, while the biggest disappointment we had to suffer this year was the defeat at the hands of Celtic in the semi-final of the Scottish Cup at Hampden. But at least the following week we had the satisfaction of ending Celtic's long-unbeaten run and prevented them from winning the title at Tynecastle.

I would imagine that 99.99 per cent of club chairmen throughout the length and breadth of the football kingdom would happily swop places with me today. And yet at the time of writing I'd just given a radio interview to a BBC reporter who asked me what it felt like to be the nearly man. On a beautiful summer's evening in Edinburgh, when I was running over in my mind all the positive things that happened in the season just gone, I must admit the question took me aback. If what we've done at Tynecastle makes me the nearly man, then there must be a queue behind me of those who are even more on the fringe of things.

My only problem during the summer, apart from how much we were going to spend and who we were going to buy, concerned the thorny issue of hooliganism that raised its ugly head at the European Championship in West Germany after we had had a warning of what was to come at the England v Scotland game at Wembley.

We as a club reserve the right to ask our supporters not to travel in Europe in season 1988/89, particularly if we are drawn against opposition from West Germany or Holland. It takes two to tango, and the problem is endemic throughout Europe. England's clubs now face at least two more years of exile from the UEFA competitions, while at the time of writing there is a question mark against England's future on the international stage.

The topic of a national membership card system has been raised, and it is now certain that the Government intend to treat the matter very seriously indeed. My personal view is that the courts have to be harder at the source of the problem – not only in sentences but in terms of withdrawing supporters' passports. People who are known trouble-makers could just as easily attach themselves to Scottish clubs in Europe, and we have to be vigilant about the mobility of these hooligans.

Football and the Government must work together to resolve the problem, which now doesn't lie so much inside the stadium but outside the ground. We are bound to suffer a knock-on effect of what happened in West Germany, since parents have seen the trouble and are sure to be concerned about their children going to matches.

At any rate, the summer was also a time when we were able to reflect that the business of the club had grown at a steady rate. We had a much better team in 1988 than in 1986, when we also finished second in the Premier Division; but the competition from other clubs last time was significantly tougher. In short, Hearts have progressed more quickly in the past five years than I could ever have anticipated.

We originally targeted St Mirren as the club we wanted to catch. Once we'd passed them our aim was to break into the top four. I think we've now passed Dundee United in terms of purchasing power, crowds and economic scale. In Aberdeen's case, the Pittodrie club is going through a transitional period in which they may have to get weaker before they get stronger. That leaves the revolutions at Parkhead and Ibrox; and in all honesty, when you examine what Billy McNeill's done for Celtic, trading and buying astutely, the Parkhead club were worthy champions in season 1987/88. Rangers seemed to buy a new player every time they met us that season, which we interpreted as the greatest compliment they could pay us.

In context, you have to look at what Hearts have achieved with the couthy approach of an outstanding management team. In the perspective of a free-spending era we've held our own pretty well, and can at the very least look towards the future with confidence and a degree of optimism: *Heart to Heart* is just the story so far.